How Church-Related Are Church-Related Colleges?

Answers Based on a Comprehensive Survey
of Supporting Constituencies of
Eighteen LCA Colleges

RICHARD W. SOLBERG
Director, Department for Higher Education
Division for Mission in North America
Lutheran Church in America

MERTON P. STROMMEN
President, Search Institute

Richard W. Solberg

BOARD OF PUBLICATION, LUTHERAN CHURCH IN AMERICA
Philadelphia
and
DIVISION FOR MISSION IN NORTH AMERICA
New York

Library of Congress Cataloging in Publication Data

Solberg, Richard W   1917–
    How church-related are church-related colleges?

    Bibliography: p.
    1.   Lutheran universities and colleges—United States.
I.   Strommen, Merton P., joint author.   II.   Title.
LC574.S64   377′.841   80–13833
ISBN 0–8006–1388–0

8035B80   Printed in the United States of America   1-1388

Contents

Contents

Acknowledgments

This book is the concluding phase of a cooperative project of the Lutheran Church in America's Division for Mission in North America and the Council of the LCA Colleges. Begun in 1973, the project has resulted in five publications: "A Statement of the Lutheran Church in America: The Basis for Partnership between Church and College"; a literature survey, *Relationships between Church-Related Colleges and Their Constituencies,* by Charles R. Bruning; the *Research Report, A Survey of Images and Expectations of LCA Colleges,* by Merton P. Strommen; and a *Technical Manual for the Research Report,* by Daniel O. Aleshire. It is impossible to acknowledge properly the contributions of time and resources made by all the institutions and individuals who participated in the successive phases of the project. Special acknowledgments are therefore limited to those directly involved in the preparation and publication of this book.

Sponsorship and oversight of the entire project has been provided by the Joint Committee of the Division for Mission in North America and the Council of the LCA Colleges: Arvin Hahn, Norman Fintel, Erno Dahl, Paul Lutz, Richard Solberg, and James Unglaube.

Valuable assistance in critiquing and editing the manuscript during various stages of its development was given by C. Gilbert Wrenn and Shelby Andress. James Unglaube developed the statistical data on college enrollments and financial support. Kenneth C. Senft, William H. Lazareth, Franklin D. Fry, and Carl T. Solberg read portions of the manuscript and offered helpful comments and suggestions.

The major task of typing and retyping successive revisions of the text was competently and patiently shared by Gerda Smith and Nadine Salvesen.

For encouragement and support at every stage of the project, for reading, listening, typing, and critiquing, my very special thanks are reserved for June N. Solberg.

For the generous financial grant which has made possible both the publishing and the distribution of this book, deep appreciation is extended to the Aid Association for Lutherans.

January 1, 1980   RICHARD W. SOLBERG

Preface

In the late 1960s and early 1970s one of America's most cherished dreams came under rude attack. Colleges and universities, for generations the focus of youthful ambition and a ladder to success, fell prey to violence and disillusion. On campuses from California to New York, long-held sacred traditions were violated as students commandeered buildings and forced the closing down of the educational process.

Most assailed and assaulted were the big universities, often the most renowned and respected, but smaller ones did not escape the onslaught. Even church-related colleges, tasting the bitterness of the times, were called before the bar of public judgment. Though none was closed down by violence, they, too, experienced disruptions. They, too, suffered some loss of esteem. Supporters who had never raised the issue before began to ask serious questions. What is distinctive about these colleges? Why should the church continue to allot its meager funds for their maintenance? Parents and students, too, watching the escalation of costs in this age of inflation, had to ask themselves whether an education at a church-related college was really worth the cost. Was the high tuition commensurate with the benefits?

The confrontations were jarring; the challenges were unsettling. But the disturbances of the 1960s had one positive result; they led both churches and colleges to reassess the purposes of their partnership. During the 1970s virtually every church-related college engaged with its supporting church body in some form of self-study, seeking to define goals, purposes, and relationships.

Factors such as these also impelled the Lutheran Church in America and its colleges to undertake a major survey among persons related to the colleges. No such formal effort had ever been made by the LCA, or indeed by any church body. It was unprecedented to inquire of a broad spectrum of constituency groups just what they

6

expected of their church-related colleges and how well their expectations were being met. Had traumas of the 1960s affected their images
and expectations? To what extent had the broad social and cultural
changes of this period influenced both colleges and constituents?

Part of the impetus for this study in the LCA was rooted in the
concern of college leaders over the erosion of church support, both
in securing dollars and in recruiting students. Further stimulus came
from occasional sharply expressed opinions that the church might
better leave the field of higher education altogether, by allowing its
colleges to become public institutions. Such a thought met strong
resistance, because educational traditions in the Lutheran church were
so closely intertwined with colleges. For many members of the LCA,
a separation between the church and its colleges was unthinkable.
What was not known was how many shared these views.

In this context of dispute and uncertainty a decision was made by
the Council of LCA Colleges and the church's Division for Mission
in North America to conduct a survey. This decision represented an
honest desire for clarification and a courageous willingness to face
reality. If the findings should be negative, it was high time to learn
the truth. If, as was earnestly hoped, the responses should be positive, there would be a dependable body of evidence with which to
meet critics of the church's mission in higher education. In either
case, both the colleges and the church would be better equipped to
plan future programs.

Assuming that a serious survey, and especially a potentially con-
troversial one, should be professionally conducted, the resources of
the Youth Research Center (now Search Institute) of Minneapolis
were engaged. The process of planning the survey, building the questionnaire, and administering it was handled with meticulous care.
Eleven groups of constituents were identified for each of the eighteen
colleges of the LCA. They included freshman and senior students,
parents of these students, trustees, administrators, faculty, alumni,
LCA clergy, synod leadership, and congregational laity. A total of
6,728 people participated and supplied usable data. Their answer
sheets were tabulated and analyzed by sophisticated statistical processes, and a research report summarizing the major findings was published in June 1976.[1]

Since then a variety of means have been employed to distribute, interpret, and publicize the results. Each college and its supporting synods received a specialized report on their own constituencies. In many cases the results were subjected to local analysis, studied in faculty and trustee workshops, conferences, or symposia. The church-wide research report continues to be reviewed and discussed in regional conferences attended by representatives of the constituency groups which participated in the original survey.

This book addresses both the church-related colleges and their constituents. It was written to encourage wider discussion of the issues examined in the research report. Its purpose is to improve the quality of communication and interaction between colleges and their supporting constituencies, and to promote better understanding of the distinctive character of the LCA colleges and of church-related colleges generally.

1
What Are Their Roots?

Since the founding of Harvard College in 1636 for the purpose of assuring the Puritan colony an educated ministry, churches and colleges have been partners in American higher education. Throughout the colonial years and especially in the nineteenth century, as America expanded westward, colleges blossomed in profusion, usually on the initiative of the clergy of one faith or another. Ten distinguished collegiate institutions were founded before 1770, either through religious initiative or with a strongly religious tone: Harvard, William and Mary, Yale, Princeton, Pennsylvania, Washington and Lee, Columbia, Brown, Rutgers, and Dartmouth. Between 1770 and the Civil War more than five hundred colleges were established, mostly under church sponsorship.[1]

Even after the passage of the Morrill Act of 1862, which provided for federal grants of public land in support of state colleges and universities, a majority of the new institutions established up to World War I continued to be church-related.

However, since the passage of the GI Bill in 1944 and the massive federal funding of college expansion during the 1950s and 1960s, the public sector has far outstripped the private sector in higher education, both in numbers of institutions and in numbers of students enrolled. By 1975 there were 3,055 collegiate institutions in the United States, of which only 739 were church-related.[2] Nevertheless, the private sector, including the church-related colleges and universities, continues to constitute a large segment of the American system of higher education. While the percentage of students enrolled in private colleges has proportionately declined, actual numbers in private and church-related colleges have slowly but steadily increased. In 1965 the 1,951,000 students in all private colleges constituted 32.9 percent of the total college enrollment. By 1977 the number of students had increased to 2,438,794, but the percentage had dropped to 21.6.[3]

No single church body has dominated the church-related sector. Virtually every denomination has entered the field and depending upon its resources and strength of commitment has supported many or few institutions. At the present time the Roman Catholics operate about 250 colleges, related in most instances to an order (e.g., Society of Jesus, Order of St. Benedict) rather than to a church diocese. United Methodists are linked to 107 colleges and universities; the two major Presbyterian bodies to 75; Southern Baptists to 53; and the United Church of Christ to 30. Lutheran colleges in the United States number 48.

Many attempts have been made to define and classify the church-related colleges, in terms of ownership and control, board membership, statements of purpose, and financial support. In their study *Church-Sponsored Higher Education in the United States,* Manning M. Pattillo and Donald M. Mackenzie (1966)[4] developed a pattern of four categories within which they classified all church-related colleges. A study by C. Robert Pace (1972)[5] for the Carnegie Commission, *Education and Evangelism,* developed another classification, and Merrimon Cunninggim (1977)[6] still another. In each case the colleges are aligned along a spectrum, ranging from close identification with a parent church on one extreme to virtual identification with the public domain on the other. According to Cunninggim, the minimum for qualifying as a church-related college is that the college claim a church connection and support this claim with observable actions that make the claim credible.[7]

An important consideration, and often a determining one, is the theological stance of the parent church with respect to higher education. For example, some may view their colleges as an educational extension of the church's evangelistic mission. Others may see them as independent institutions, in partnership with the church, whose task is to contribute through educational programs to the enhancement of human dignity and well-being.

Other factors help shape the character and climate of individual church-related colleges. One often finds that location, ethnic roots, size, faculty, and student clientele have helped produce great differences, even among the colleges of a single denomination.

LUTHERAN HIGHER EDUCATION
COMES TO AMERICA

One purpose of this book is to identify the images and expectations of groups of people in some way related to the colleges of the Lutheran Church in America. It addresses these questions: What do these groups see as essential in a church-related college? To what extent are their expectations being met?

Findings are best understood when viewed in context. Therefore, it will be helpful to learn something about the colleges involved in the study and about their historical traditions.

Since the German Reformation of the sixteenth century, the Lutheran church has given strong emphasis to the importance of education at all levels. Martin Luther himself was a product of the medieval university system, gaining a doctorate in Bible and the honor of a professorial chair in Wittenberg University. Not only was he concerned for the religious education of the young, as evidenced in his writing of the Small and Large Catechisms, but he was concerned also for general education through publicly supported schools. This he stressed when addressing the princes of Germany. Luther viewed the university both as a guarantor of a clergy learned in the Scriptures and as a promoter and patron of culture. The close ties between church and university which have persisted in Germany until now bear witness to similar convictions among Luther's followers. Most Lutheran pastors in Germany still receive their theological preparation in state universities.

The Lutheran tradition of education was brought to America by immigrant groups of differing national origins, speaking many different languages. Swedish and Dutch immigrants who settled along the Delaware River in the early 1600s and Germans who responded to William Penn's invitations in the late 1600s were followed in the early 1700s by still larger German migrations that moved into upper New York, Pennsylvania, and down the Great Valley of Virginia into the Carolinas.

In the nineteenth century the United States expanded territorially across the entire continent, as it received immigrants from every part of Europe, as well as Asia and Africa. New waves of Germans entered the Midwest, finding homes in Ohio, Illinois, Wisconsin, and Missouri. Scandinavians from Norway, Sweden, Denmark, and Finland brought with them not only their language and ethnic tradition but also their Lutheran faith. Under the leadership of clergy who accompanied the migrations or were sent later by European churches, congregations were organized almost as soon as homes were built and fields planted. Associations of congregations and pastors followed, and eventually schools, colleges, and seminaries.[8]

Lutheran church history in America has been characterized by a process, often irregular and fraught with conflict, of drawing together these widely scattered groups, with their diverse languages, into common structures called synods. These synods merged into larger denominational groups, and gradually, over 150 years, formed three major Lutheran denominations: The Lutheran Church in America (LCA), The American Lutheran Church (ALC), and The Lutheran Church—Missouri Synod (LC-MS).

Synodical mergers were occasionally accompanied by institutional mergers, but more frequently the new church organization adopted the educational offspring of its predecessors. The three major Lutheran groups today relate to forty-two colleges. Of these, seventeen are primarily affiliated with the LCA, eleven with the ALC, and thirteen with the LC-MS. One is jointly operated by the LCA and ALC.

THE LCA FAMILY OF COLLEGES

One may classify the colleges of the LCA according to historical traditions, employing both ecclesiastical and ethnic dimensions. The colleges which were products of the "old" Lutheran influx of the colonial period are largely concentrated in the eastern states. Later migrations into Ohio, Illinois, and Nebraska resulted in the establishment of colleges in these states. Eleven of the present eighteen LCA colleges were founded in the sixty-year span between 1832 and 1891: Gettysburg, Roanoke, Wittenberg, Carthage, Muhlenberg, Newberry, Susquehanna, Thiel, Wagner, Midland, and Lenoir-Rhyne. They were a part of the institutional dowry which the United Lutheran Church in America brought into the 1962 merger which formed the LCA.

Four LCA colleges—Augustana, Bethany, Gustavus Adolphus, and Upsala—come out of the Augustana Lutheran Church, a tradition brought to the United States by Swedish immigrants in the mid-nineteenth century.

The Danes and Finns, who joined with the Augustana Lutheran Church and the ULCA to form the LCA in 1962, each brought a college into the merged church: Grand View and Suomi, respectively. California Lutheran College was founded in 1959 as a joint venture of several Lutheran groups in the Pacific Southwest.

It should be no surprise that the collegiate institutions emerging from this kind of historical and ethnic diversity are not alike in spirit or character. Their enrollments vary from 440 to 2,600 students. Their ages vary from 21 to 148 years. They are found in widely separated locations, from Southern California to Staten Island, New York, and from South Carolina to the northern peninsula of Michigan. Their student clienteles vary academically and socially, as well as in identification with the Christian faith. Their admission policies and graduation requirements differ significantly, and in 1979–80 their basic charges for a year of study ranged from $3,440 to $6,200.

Yet as "colleges of the LCA" they share some very substantial bonds. They are all essentially undergraduate liberal arts institutions, offering major concentrations in the traditional areas of human knowledge, with a strong emphasis on preprofessional and professional studies. All are small institutions which offer the opportunity for close personal relationships between faculty and students. If one of Cunninggim's classifications of church-related colleges were used, they would probably be aligned with "proclaiming colleges." In Cunninggim's scheme, this broad middle sector of the spectrum embraces institutions that see themselves as academic partners of the church. A college so classified, he says, knows itself first "as a college, not a religious institution. . . . But as a college, it is in confederation with the church and is glad to admit it."[9]

The eighteen LCA colleges are a resource of formidable proportions. In 1979–80 they enrolled a total of 24,275 full-time students (plus over 5,000 part-time students), of whom 27 percent were Lutherans. Full-time faculty totaled 1,492. In 1978 students paid a total of $111,000,000 in tuition, fees, board, and room charges. This accounted for 77 percent of the total cost for a year's education. The remaining costs were made up through endowments, gifts, and grants from a variety of sources.

13

Of the total expenditure of $137,000,000 (1978–79) for the eighteen colleges, $2,438,538 (or approximately 1.8 percent) came from LCA synods, and $3,678,000 (2.7 percent) came from college endowments. These combined endowments totaled $85,648,202.

In 1978–79 financial aid in the amount of $42,516,574 was administered to 69 percent of all students, for an average of $2,538 per recipient. Grant and scholarship funds totaled $27,394,348, of which the colleges themselves provided approximately $9,500,000.

Total assets of the colleges in 1978–79, including plant value, were $474,150,000. It is interesting that the total of college expenditures equaled the combined expenditures of one-third of the 6,100 congregations of the LCA.[10]

CHURCH AND COLLEGE AS PARTNERS

In the structure of the LCA, a denomination of 3,100,000 members, institutional relationship and support is the primary responsibility of its thirty-three synods. Though the denomination extends official recognition and provides a variety of services to its colleges, the operational grants given annually are made by the synods territorially related to each college.

Every synod is expected to support at least one college and to elect some of its members to the college board of trustees. In most cases ownership of the college is vested in a board rather than in the synod. All colleges and their supporting synods have adopted "statements of intent." These documents, subject to periodic review, describe the relationship between college and synod and their mutual expectations and commitments.

To assist the colleges and synods in such a review, the LCA approved a basic statement on higher education at its biennial convention in 1976: "The Basis for Partnership between Church and College."[11] The Partnership Statement finds its theological base in a recognition of the God-ordained validity of the "orders of preservation," those natural and cultural structures which give form and purpose to individual and collective human life. It affirms that God is the Lord of *all* creation and that its ultimate governance and preservation is in his hands. He provides for the temporal guidance and care of human society through institutions such as the family, government, schools, hospitals, business and commerce, and the arts.

Those persons who acknowledge God's revelation through Jesus Christ are united as the people of God in the institution of the church. Here they worship him, are sustained through his gifts of Word and Sacrament, and are equipped for lives of service.

They are not, however, separated from the rest of the world in a kind of antiseptic isolation. As Christian people, they are also called to a life of thankful service to God and their neighbors. They may happily join forces with all persons of goodwill, whether Christian or not, to improve the quality of human life and to promote justice in all segments of society.

Understandably, the church must direct its limited temporal resources where funds will be used most effectively to achieve its purposes. Once provision has been made for its essential ministry of Word and Sacrament, the church historically has stressed activity in two great areas of human service: healing and teaching. In its teaching ministry, it has been not only the dispenser of religious doctrine but also the patron and sponsor of disciplines that enrich the mind and the spirit: the arts, humanities, and sciences.

The Partnership Statement of the LCA affirms boldly that education in general and church-related colleges in particular have an integrity and a purpose grounded in God's created order that finds expression in the First Article of the Apostles' Creed.

According to this credo, the LCA as a denomination does not support colleges as evangelistic centers or parochial schools. Rather, it sees its colleges as educational institutions related to, but distinct from, the church. Their primary purpose is rooted in an honest desire to help young people become more sensitive and competent citizens who will seek to promote justice and the common good. In a world of deteriorating public morals and ethical standards, the Lutheran Church in America welcomes and shares this kind of service by its colleague institutions as one of the most critical in our society today.

COLLEGE VIGNETTES

Each of the eighteen colleges of the LCA is a distinctive institution, with a character and history quite its own. They were founded for a variety of reasons, in a variety of locations by a variety of persons. The common denominator was simply that most of the founders were members of the Lutheran church.

The constituencies of these eighteen colleges supplied the data on which this book is based. On some topics the responses for all colleges were similar. On others there were notable differences. A series of brief descriptive vignettes of the colleges may aid in an understanding of why and how some similarities and differences might occur.[12]

The "Old" Lutheran Tradition in America

GETTYSBURG. The oldest of LCA colleges is Gettysburg College, located in a small town on the edge of the great Civil War battlefield in south-central Pennsylvania. Founded as Pennsylvania College in 1832 by a group of Lutheran laymen and clergy, it has been an independent institution from its beginning. Ownership is vested in its thirty-eight member board of trustees, a majority of whom are required to be Lutherans and eight of whom are elected by the Central Pennsylvania and Maryland synods.

Gettysburg College maintains high academic standards and has for many years limited its enrollment to approximately 2,000 students, drawn mostly from Pennsylvania, New York, and New Jersey. The college has provided pretheological education for more than five hundred present members of the LCA clergy, more than any other college. Academic programs are conservative, strongly emphasizing the liberal arts. Approximately 17 percent of the students are Lutherans.

ROANOKE. The second oldest college is Roanoke, located in Salem, Virginia, in the Blue Ridge Mountains of the southwestern part of that state. Founded in 1842 by two Lutheran ministers, it enjoys high esteem among the private liberal arts colleges of the Old Dominion. Located as it is in a state with a small Lutheran population, Roanoke also has a small percentage of Lutheran students (9.6 percent in 1979). About 800 of its 1,350 students are Virginians, but it draws 17 percent of its enrollment from the northern states of Pennsylvania, New York, and Connecticut. There is a strong bond of loyalty to the college in the Virginia Synod, though the ownership of the college is vested in a board of trustees.

WITTENBERG. Founded in 1845 by Lutherans who had moved west from Pennsylvania and Maryland, Wittenberg College represented a conscious effort to Americanize a European tradition. Located in Springfield, Ohio, it is now the largest of the LCA institutions, having also in 1959 adopted a university structure. Most of its

2,600 students are in the College of Arts and Sciences, but the School of Music, Hamma Divinity School (until its recent merger and reorganization as Trinity Seminary, in Columbus, Ohio), and the School of Community Education have extended the services of the university beyond the conventional limits of the liberal arts. International studies are among its special curricular emphases. Wittenberg has traditionally placed a high value on academic performance, and in recent years it has also made a purposeful effort to strengthen its character as a Lutheran university. About 25 percent of its present student body are Lutherans, mostly drawn from the territories of its supporting synods of Ohio and Indiana-Kentucky.

CARTHAGE. Carthage College, founded in 1847 in downstate Illinois, enjoys the unusual distinction of looking back on the troubled 1960s and early 1970s as the decade in which it made a successful transition to a new location in Kenosha, Wisconsin, overlooking Lake Michigan, constructed a complete educational plant to accommodate its 1,500 students, and more than doubled its endowment. It is the only college of either the LCA or The American Lutheran Church in Wisconsin, a heavily Lutheran state, and while primarily related to the LCA and its two synods in Wisconsin and Michigan, it also maintains a cooperative relationship with the ALC. Forty-six percent of its students are Lutheran.

MUHLENBERG. Named for the "father of American Lutheranism," Henry Melchior Muhlenberg, Muhlenberg College was founded in 1848 in Allentown, Pennsylvania, as a college for men. Since 1957 it has been coeducational. Maintaining high academic standards and conservative academic programming, it has limited its enrollment to approximately 1,500 full-time students and has developed a strong premedical program with an enviable record in the placing of its graduates in medical schools. A majority of its trustees are selected by its supporting synods, Northeastern and Southeastern Pennsylvania and Slovak Zion. Located in northeastern Pennsylvania, Muhlenberg also draws heavily on both New Jersey and New York for its students, only 15 percent of whom are Lutheran.

NEWBERRY. Founded in 1856 by the Lutheran Synod of South Carolina and Adjacent States, Newberry College is the most southern of LCA schools, both geographically and in its campus climate. With an enrollment of 900, it is one of four LCA colleges with fewer than

1,000 students. Virtually all its students, 24 percent of whom are Lutheran, are drawn from south of Virginia. Notable is the fact that 13 percent of Newberry's students are black, the second highest percentage of any LCA college. Two-thirds of its trustees are elected by the three supporting synods: South Carolina, Southeastern, and Florida.

SUSQUEHANNA. Susquehanna University was established in 1858 at Selinsgrove, virtually in the center of the state of Pennsylvania, as a seminary for the training of Lutheran missionaries. It remained very small until the 1950s, and since then has grown steadily to its present enrollment of 1,450 full-time students. It has especially strong departments of music and business administration and operates an extensive program of field internships to assist students in career selection and job placement. Most of the thirty-nine trustees are elected by the college board, which also is the legal owner of the college. The supporting Central Pennsylvania Synod elects eight of the trustees.

THIEL. The most western of Lutheran colleges in Pennsylvania, and the latest to be founded in that state, is Thiel College. Organized in 1866 through the initiative of William A. Passavant, institutional godfather of the former Pittsburgh Synod, the college was located in Greenville, Pennsylvania, in 1870. The relationship between the college and the church has historically been very close, most of the pastors of the Western Pennsylvania–West Virginia Synod having received their college degrees at Thiel. Most of its 1,050 students are from Pennsylvania, with smaller but equal numbers from Ohio, New York, and New Jersey. The early tradition of the college was classical, but in recent years the natural sciences and business have largely replaced languages and literature. Lutheran enrollment is about 21 percent. The synod elects a majority of the trustees.

WAGNER. Located on Staten Island, overlooking New York harbor, Wagner College was organized in 1883. Its enrollment of more than 2,500 reflects the cosmopolitan character of its environment. Most of its students are from New York, and a large percentage are commuters. The predominant student population is Roman Catholic, and about 10 percent are black, Asian, or Hispanic, while 7 percent are Lutheran. The college has a large part-time enrollment, mostly involved in graduate programs in business administration or education. Among its other special programs, Wagner offers a baccalaureate degree in nursing and operates an overseas study center in Bregenz, Austria. Though recognized as a college of the LCA and related to the New York synods, Wagner is a fully independent institution, its board of trustees electing all of its own members.

MIDLAND LUTHERAN. Midland Lutheran College was founded in 1883 in Atchison, Kansas, later moving to its present location in Fremont, Nebraska. In 1962 it was joined by Luther College of Wahoo, Nebraska, a junior college of the Augustana Lutheran Church, thus epitomizing the merger which formed the Lutheran Church in America in the same year. The composition of Midland's student enrollment also reflects the character of its social environment. About 650 of its 800 students are residents of Nebraska, 56 percent are Lutheran (the highest percentage of any LCA college), and slightly more than 3 percent are black. A majority of the board of trustees are elected by the Nebraska and Rocky Mountain synods.

LENOIR-RHYNE. Lenoir-Rhyne College, located in Hickory, North Carolina, was founded by Lutheran ministers as à degree-granting college in 1891, but it has roots in several earlier institutions. The college is owned by the North Carolina Synod, the third-oldest Lutheran synod in the United States, which elects all members of the college's board of trustees. Its close ties with the college are also expressed in generous financial support. Although the great majority of its 1,300 students are from North Carolina, Lenoir-Rhyne does draw from neighboring southern states and also from the Northeast. Thirty percent are Lutheran. Within its regular liberal arts curriculum, Lenoir-Rhyne has developed a comprehensive program for the education of the hearing-impaired.

The Swedish Tradition

When the Augustana Lutheran Church, of Swedish origins, entered the merger which formed the LCA in 1962, it brought with it four vigorous collegiate institutions, each of which bore the distinctive marks of its heritage. These colleges were the products of the mid-nineteenth-century Swedish Lutheran immigration. The older colonial groups of Swedes, which had settled along the Delaware River in the 1630s, had long since lost their Lutheran identity and been absorbed by the Episcopalians.

AUGUSTANA. Northern Illinois became the first focus of the new groups, and it was in Chicago in 1860 that Augustana College was founded. In 1875, both the college and the theological seminary found permanent location in Rock Island, Illinois, on the banks of the Mississippi River. Here, under able intellectual and spiritual leadership, Augustana became the capital of Swedish Lutheranism in America. Its present enrollment of more than 2,400 students is largely drawn from Illinois, including substantial numbers from metropolitan Chicago, as attested to by the strong representation of Roman Catholic and black students. One-third of its students are Lutheran. Academic programs are strong and varied, and graduates have achieved particular recognition in the fields of geography, geology, and music, as well as theology. Augustana's close relationship with the Illinois Synod is reflected in the substantial financial support it receives and in the strong participation of synod membership on the college board of trustees. Because of its earlier affiliation with the Augustana Synod, which was national rather than regional in structure, Augustana's alumni are geographically more widely dispersed than those of many other colleges of the LCA.

GUSTAVUS ADOLPHUS. Many of the characteristics attributed to Augustana could be applied to the other large midwestern college formerly related to the Augustana Synod, Gustavus Adolphus. The product of Swedish migration into Minnesota, Gustavus was founded in 1862 at St. Peter, Minnesota. Throughout the years, Minnesota has been the heartland of Scandinavian Lutheran strength, both Swedish and Norwegian. Gustavus clearly reflects this ethnic dimension. Of its 2,300 students, 50 percent are Lutheran, giving it the second highest concentration of Lutheran students of any LCA college. From the Minnesota and Red River Valley synods it also enjoys the most substantial financial support of any LCA college. In addition to its generally strong academic program, Gustavus has fostered its ethnic heritage. An outstanding expression of this is the annual Nobel Conference held in cooperation with the Nobel Foundation in Sweden, which brings Nobel prize winners to the campus each year as lecturers and seminar leaders.

BETHANY. Another college of Swedish Lutheran origin which has brought a rich cultural dimension into the LCA is Bethany College. Founded in 1881 by a Lutheran pastor in the small rural Swedish community of Lindsborg, Kansas, Bethany has become a center for the musical and visual arts, as well as an example of a well-managed small liberal arts college. It receives support from the Central States, Rocky Mountain, and Texas-Louisiana synods. Of its 900 students, most from Kansas or Colorado, 42 percent are Lutheran. On the Bethany campus is a major art museum, reflecting the creative work of a Swedish-born artist, Birger Sandzen, who established a strong fine arts program at the college and for fifty years inspired his students with his own paintings of Kansas landscapes. Virtually since the founding of the college, an annual presentation of the *Messiah* has been performed by a chorus drawn from Lindsborg and neighboring communities. More than three thousand persons now attend performances, which have been expanded into a week-long series of oratorios and cantatas, attracting soloists of national reputation.

UPSALA. Illustrative of the dramatic way in which the colleges of the LCA are conditioned by their social and cultural environment is Upsala College. Also of Swedish Lutheran origin, and bearing the name of one of Sweden's great universities, this college was founded in Brooklyn, New York, in 1893, in what was then a strong Swedish community. Now located in East Orange, New Jersey, well within the bounds of the metropolitan area including New York City, Newark, Hoboken, and Jersey City, Upsala serves the most characteristically urban community of all LCA colleges. Of its 1,200 full-time students, 24 percent are black or Hispanic, and a very small percentage are Lutheran. The college operates a highly respected academic program, with a strong community orientation. A majority of its trustees are elected by the New Jersey and New England synods.

The Danish Tradition

GRAND VIEW. A third ethnic stream which entered the LCA at its formation in 1962 was Danish in its origin. Flavoring this particular group, which founded Grand View College in 1896 in Des Moines, Iowa, was the spirit of Nicolai F. S. Grundtvig, pastor and leader of the folk-school movement in Denmark.

For many years Grand View College operated as a junior college, but recent accreditation by the North Central Association established it as a baccalaureate institution. Its first four-year program leads to a professional degree in nursing. Grand View projects its future curricular development with an emphasis on professional programs

21

rather than a duplication of the strongly liberal arts emphasis of most Lutheran colleges. Most of its 1,150 students are off-campus residents of Des Moines, almost 300 of them attending part-time. Its enrollment of 107 foreign students ranks it with Wagner as a leader among LCA colleges. Seventy-eight students, or 9.1 percent of its enrollment, are members of American minority groups. Thirteen percent of the students are Lutheran. A majority of the college trustees are elected by the Iowa Synod.

The Finnish Tradition

SUOMI. The only two-year institution related to the LCA is Suomi College, located in Hancock, Michigan, and founded in 1896. Before the merger forming the LCA, Hancock was also the headquarters of the Finnish Lutheran body called the Suomi Synod and of its theological seminary. Present enrollment at the college is 440, 22 percent of which is Lutheran. It is a stated college policy to seek to enroll disadvantaged young people and to develop programs that will enable them to qualify for further college study or for paraprofessional positions. The college also has developed cross-cultural programs, involving black students from metropolitan Detroit and groups of students from the U.S. trust territories of Micronesia. Church support to Suomi is provided by the LCA's Division for Mission in North America, which also participates in the nomination and election of a majority of its board of trustees.

A Recent Venture

CALIFORNIA LUTHERAN. The youngest of the colleges affiliated with the LCA is California Lutheran College. It was founded in 1959 at Thousand Oaks, California, in order to provide Lutheran educational opportunity in the Pacific Southwest. The American Lutheran Church and the Pacific Southwest Synod of the LCA provide financial support and share equally in the election of members of the college board. Enrollments in recent years have been steadily increasing. Presently attending are 1,430 full-time students. An extensive part-time program consisting largely of graduate students brings the total enrollment to almost 2,500. Forty-six percent of the full-time students are Lutheran. One of the special programs of the college lays stress on lifelong learning and includes a preschool laboratory and a Senior Fellows Program, under which retired persons are invited to spend a limited term as residents. They participate in college life and offer services in their particular area of expertise, whether academic, administrative, or technical.

SUMMARY

These are the institutions of the LCA among which the survey of images and expectations was conducted. Over the course of a century and a half they have provided their communities and the nation with a stream of graduates who have entered virtually every field of human enterprise: professional, cultural, civic, and international. They have enriched thousands of Lutheran congregations with both lay and clergy leadership. In the minds of broad segments of church membership, they have been virtually synonymous with the church itself.

True to their heritage, Lutherans have supported these institutions, faithfully sacrificing to send their sons and daughters there to earn the college degree which would open the door to a life richer and better than their own. In most instances they left the formulation of goals and programs to trusted academic and ecclesiastical leaders. As most Americans, they believed colleges were good, but they supported these particular institutions because they were operated by the church, not because of any eloquent statements of purpose approved by synods or offered for scrutiny by a broader constituency.

But as these colleges entered the 1950s and 1960s and shouldered a larger share of the public burden of higher education, changes began to occur in program and clientele which raised questions of institutional direction and character in the mind of many a loyal supporter.

The following chapters are meant to state many of these questions frankly and to ascertain whether the constituencies are really satisfied with the direction their colleges seem to be taking in the new age of American higher education. Such an inquiry properly begins with their expectations of college goals and purposes.

2
What Are Their Goals?

During the 1950s and 1960s, leaders in education and politics were more concerned with telling the American public what it should want than with asking what the public expected of its colleges and universities. Alexander W. Astin, in the September 1977 issue of *Change*,[1] points out that virtually all the major public decisions affecting higher education during these years were being made on economic or political, rather than educational, grounds. Beginning with Sputnik in 1957, the need to bolster American international prestige and to develop technology and manpower in specialized fields deemed essential to the national interest became the motivation for the revision and expansion of the structure and substance of the entire American educational system, from elementary through graduate schools.

Liberal arts colleges, church-related institutions among them, joined universities and state and community colleges in the rush for public funds that became available for buildings, personnel, and equipment during the 1950s and 1960s. Often little thought was given to the educational impact of new programs and policies on the college. Only under the traumatic impact of the student revolts of the 1960s did serious reevaluation begin. An added incentive to take stock came in the Carnegie Commission's 1973 finding that "critical evaluation of society for the sake of society's renewal"[2] was one of the major purposes of higher education. Colleges and their constituents, however, were obliged to ask whether their institutions were really in a position to contribute much to such a process of renewal.

Evaluation that might lead to renewal was one of the concerns that led to the decision in the LCA to conduct a survey of images and expectations. Among all the areas to evaluate and the questions raised by the hundreds of constituents, none seemed as important as those dealing with goals.

What did these persons expect their colleges to achieve in the lives

24

of the students entrusted to them for four precious years? And to what extent were their expectations being met? To answer both these questions, persons taking the survey were asked two questions regarding each of a series of goal statements:

1. How desirable is the stated goal for your college? (Response possibilities were: "absolutely essential," "very desirable," "quite desirable," "somewhat desirable," "neither desirable nor undesirable," "undesirable," and "very undesirable.")

2. How well is the stated goal being achieved at your college? (Response possibilities were: "very well," "quite well," "somewhat," "very little," "not at all," "no longer," and "don't know.")

Six goal expectations emerge as common to the widely divergent college constituency groups. They were derived empirically by a factor analysis of the answers of 6,728 respondents to each of the thirty-six goal statements in the questionnaire. This highly sensitive method discerns the constructs or commonly held attitudes that cause people to answer items in certain consistent ways. Here it yielded six meaningful clusters of goal statements, each of which focuses on a broad goal expectation.

The six broad goals represent the dimensions of a college education which, according to a substantial majority of all constituency groups, are of key importance. Listed here, in order of indicated desirability and with the percentages of all respondents who viewed them as either "absolutely essential" or "highly desirable," they are:

Preparation for Life	79%
Wholeness of Person	78%
Liberal Arts Education	75%
Christian Perspective	59%
Social Change	58%
Religious Diversity	47%

What does each of these goals involve?

"Preparation for Life" stresses preparation for one's future work, mastery of a subject-matter field, and the development of future leaders in society.

"Wholeness of Person" is a concept involving such components as self-understanding, sense of community, developing potential, attitudes toward learning, and cross-cultural sensitivity.

The "Liberal Arts Education" goal includes such elements as cul-

25

tural appreciation, imaginative and analytical thinking, general academic excellence, and desire for lifelong learning.

"Christian Perspective" is the goal of growth in faith and personal commitment to Christ, an understanding of Christ's teachings, and an academic setting for the Christian scholar.

"Social Change" is the goal of concern for human welfare and the development of understanding and skills for producing social change, rather than direct social action.

"Religious Diversity" is the appreciation of a religiously diversified faculty and student body, not necessarily all Christian, while maintaining a Christian orientation of the college, with free and vigorous dialogue on matters of belief.

These six expectations show that among constituencies of all LCA colleges, including both "producers" and "consumers," there is quite general agreement as to what a church-related college should offer its students. Constituents of LCA colleges want their colleges to be student-centered institutions that give adequate recognition to the intellectual, social, and spiritual dimensions of each young person's development. They do not wish their colleges to be parochial, either religiously or socially, but do want them to provide a climate for growth in religious faith and personal commitment to Christ. While preparation for future occupations and professions is important, LCA colleges are seen not as job-training schools but as institutions seeking first of all to educate persons in a liberal arts tradition.

If expectations such as these are not fully realized, neither the institutions themselves nor the church which supports them can be faulted for aiming too low. Such expectations reflect a deeply rooted concern in the Lutheran church and among the Lutheran college constituencies in general for enriching the quality of life for members of the human family and for the shaping of a more responsible and humane society. It is encouraging that in the face of widespread uncertainty and confusion on the American scene concerning educational goals, or even the value of a college education, LCA college constituents share a common understanding of the purpose of a church-related liberal arts college.

High goals, however, tend to defy full achievement. While recognizing this fact and the risk of such an evaluation, the survey asked the same constituents to indicate their perception of how well each goal was being achieved. In computing the disparity between expectations and perceptions, all "don't know" answers were excluded. This procedure gave assurance that only those who felt they had some basis for judgment were included in the calculation of disparity scores. However, it did substantially reduce the size of the samples, because an average of 40 percent of the respondents gave a "don't know" answer to one or more items in the six goals scales. This apparent lack of an informed base for judgment among a substantial portion of the constituencies is instructive for both college and church regarding the need for more information about one's college and first-hand contact with campus activities. Among those who did venture an evaluation, judgments of the colleges' success vary in degree, depending upon which goal was being considered and which group was responding.

In dealing with the whole matter of expectations and outcomes, it is important to exercise certain cautions. In his comprehensive study of student attitudes and behavior, *The Four Critical Years* (1977), Alexander Astin[3] reminds us that many of the outcomes sought by colleges and often stated as institutional goals are long-range in character and not attainable in a four-year span.

Moreover, Astin reminds us that many of the changes that take place in student attitudes and behavior are related as much to a maturing process as to the college exposure and would occur whether a person is in college or not. It is therefore not easy to sort out and evaluate the specific impact of the college experience, especially in such noncognitive areas as attitudes and behavior.

WHOLENESS OF PERSON

Ranked consistently high by all the groups, but especially by faculty and college administrators, is the expectation that the college should actively seek to educate in such a way that a student's growth as a whole person may be enhanced, in noncognitive as well as cognitive areas. Four out of five regard this as an "absolutely essential" or "very desirable" goal for a church-related college.

The general assessment of success in achieving this goal, as measured on the seven-point scale used in the survey instrument, was 4.72, indicating that the goal is being "somewhat" achieved. The mean for the corresponding expectation scale was 6.03. The performance rating of the LCA colleges as a whole in meeting this high expectation may provide cause for some dissatisfaction.

Among those whose rating shows least satisfaction with what has been achieved with respect to this goal are the faculty, administrative leaders, and college seniors. These on-campus groups who have worked together over long periods of time display a healthy recognition that goals of this kind are not short-term in character but rather qualitative lifelong goals in the pursuit of which the college experience, however crucial, is only a single chapter.

Contrasting with them are freshman students, and especially their parents, who assume, or perhaps hope, that the goal is being achieved very well. For many of these persons the college experience has been eagerly awaited, surrounded with dreams, and a sensitive questionnaire shows their perceptions to be quite removed from reality.

A reassuring note of general satisfaction comes from the church leadership and the laity who form the heart of congregational support. In their judgment, differences between images and expectations are minimal with respect to the goal "Wholeness of Person."

PREPARATION FOR LIFE

A related expectation, that the college should prepare students for life, also ranks very high for all groups. Responses to items in the scale, however, show a marked difference in emphasis among certain groups. Students tend to stress preparation for specific jobs and occupations. Pastors emphasize the importance of developing competent leaders for society. Parents rank all items in this scale high, but give preference to leadership development over job preparation.

Among the 60 percent of the total sample who feel able to assess the success of the colleges in achieving this goal, general satisfaction is indicated. Sweeping claims, however, ought to be studiously avoided, because these goals are complex and many-faceted. What is being assessed is not the actual level of achievement of a college but the perceptions of people. These may be based upon astute and informed observation or upon ephemeral personal impressions or images. Nevertheless, what people think or feel to be true is frequently as important as the truth itself.

Senior students, for whom preparation for life leans heavily in the direction of job preparation, provide the most significant example of disparity between what they want and what they have realized for themselves. Their parents, probably reflecting a broader understanding of life and a longer perspective than their impatient offspring, indicate general satisfaction with the role played by the college in preparing their son or daughter for life.

Laity in the congregations, especially those between the ages of thirty-six and fifty-one, the age-group probably most shocked by the social disorders of the 1960s, rank second to the seniors in registering disappointment with how this goal is being achieved. On the other hand, pastors of the LCA, whose expectations are somewhat lower than average, express above-average satisfaction with the way their colleges are preparing students for life.

LIBERAL ARTS EDUCATION

The third expectation, "Liberal Arts Education," is a traditional goal for church-related colleges. However, agreement concerning its meaning and content has always been elusive, even among college faculties. The most notable variations in how importantly this goal is viewed appear between the professional educators and nonprofessionals. Remembering that 75 percent of the entire sample regard liberal arts education as either "absolutely essential" or "very desirable," and that only 2.3 percent describe it in unfavorable terms, it should be clear that the variations are not great. As might be expected, college faculty, administrators, and trustees are the most ardent champions of the liberal arts. Pastors are also strong supporters, while the laity display least enthusiasm. Students, surprisingly, outrank only the three groups of congregational laity. Seniors rank well above freshmen, which suggests that the four-year college experience has tended to increase student appreciation for the values of a liberal arts education.

None of the declared goals of LCA colleges show a greater range in disparity scores than is evident for this goal. The college faculty especially, but also administrative leaders, feel keenly that their ideal is far from being achieved. The failure of their college and students to achieve the high goals of cultural appreciation, imaginative and analytical thinking, intellectual curiosity, and discipline remains a matter of deep concern for faculty and administrators. Such dissatisfaction may actually be the mark of college leaders who have not yielded to complacency and mediocrity but are ever seeking to enhance this dimension of their education program.

Except for senior students, none of the other groups manifests this concern. In general, they see their college providing a good liberal arts education that rivals or exceeds their expectations. Freshman students and their parents, who rank the importance of a liberal arts education slightly below the averages of other groups, indicate that what they find being offered is far better than they had expected.

CHRISTIAN PERSPECTIVE

Although six out of ten respondents deem it "absolutely essential" or "very desirable" that the college help students adopt or sharpen a life perspective centering in Christianity, many view this goal as less important. Substantial differences can be found in the expectations that characterize some constituent groups.

Pastors and synod leaders understandably are the most eager of all groups that their college encourage growth and development in Christian commitment and theological understanding. Faculty, while less emphatic, still offer strong support, with more than half strongly affirming that the college should provide opportunities for growth in the Christian faith.

Almost half the total faculty sample (45 percent) describe as "absolutely essential" or "very desirable" the expectation that the college should help students affirm a personal commitment to Christ. If the categories "quite desirable" and "somewhat desirable" were included, another 35 percent would be added. That such expectations may be freely and even strongly expressed by many of the classroom teachers in the colleges of the LCA is in itself illustrative of one of the distinctive characteristics of a church-related institution. Such expectations of a college would neither be entertained nor expressed, perhaps even by these same faculty members, if they were teaching in publicly supported institutions.

Although neither freshmen nor seniors place this expectation among their highest, it is significant to take note of their actual percentage responses. Fifty-four percent of freshman students come to colleges of the LCA with a strong expectation ("absolutely essential'" or "very desirable") that the college will help them affirm their personal commitment to Christ. Forty-seven percent of the seniors approach graduation four years later still strongly convinced that this is a proper expectation of their college. With respect to the expectation that their college should provide opportunities for growth in the Christian faith, the percentages are even higher, namely, 65 percent for freshmen and 57 percent for seniors.

Young persons of college age are not likely to display their spiritual needs and hungers for all to see, at the very time of their lives when they are eagerly seeking social and intellectual acceptance and approval from peers and professors. A great measure of sensitivity and understanding is required of colleges that enroll these young men and women. They come with high hopes but often well-concealed concerns and expectations. Reflection on the religious expectation of six thousand freshmen who enter the eighteen colleges of the LCA each fall might result in some alteration of the pattern and context of many campus programs, both academic and nonacademic.

Within the broadly stated expectation that a church-related college should provide an educational program with a Christian perspective, there are many views of what such a perspective really means and how it is manifested. Responses to single items in the survey make this abundantly clear.

For some, the desired accent is to seek growth in knowledge and Christian faith. For others it is to encourage dialogue and interaction between theology and other disciplines in the college, as well as inquiry into religious and ethical questions. For such persons the college should be a place for genuine encounter between religious faith and secular learning, where each enhances the other. It is significant that for questionnaire items embodying these expectations, the average responses for all eleven groups range between "quite desirable" and "very desirable." Pastors, trustees, and older laity identify most favorably with expectations such as these which help students into a "Christian Perspective." This strong interest of noncampus constituents could prove a fruitful area for involving administrative and faculty leaders in LCA colleges in dialogue with clergy and thoughtful parish laity. Such conversations would increase a sense of rapport between leaders of college and congregation.

It is highly significant that people who are supportive of a religious perspective in the life and program of a college do not always agree theologically on the nature of that perspective. Some conceive of the college as an extension of the congregation, using an academic setting for carrying out the basic role of the church. Such persons view their college as carrying the responsibility of proclaiming the gospel of God's redemptive grace through Jesus Christ for human salvation. For them the rationale of a church-related college is evangelism.

Others see the college as an educational institution distinct in its basic purpose from that of the church. As a partner its task is to teach, lead students into the mysteries of the created world, and enhance and enrich the lives of people, firmly convinced that it is thereby serving both God and society.

Both these views are represented among the supporters of LCA colleges. This is clearly attested to by the responses of 6,728 people to the item, "The college differs from the church in that its primary task is not redemption, but rather to focus on the truth about creation."

LCA clergy are almost equally divided on this question, 45 percent expressing agreement and 40 percent disagreement. Fourteen percent are uncertain. Such differences suggest both the need and the desirability of ongoing discussion concerning the theological basis for and the nature of LCA's institutional involvement in higher education.

With respect to how well LCA colleges achieve the goal "Christian Perspective" for their students, the clergy register judgments similar to those of college faculties and administrators regarding the goal "Liberal Arts Education." In both instances the goals are dear to the hearts and professions of these groups. Hence, their expectations are very high. It should be no surprise that neither group is prepared to settle for less than superior performance.

Joining the clergy in the pattern of high expectations and accompanying dissatisfaction with the colleges' efforts toward student growth in Christian commitment and theological perception are synod board members. Some disparity between image and expectation also exists for older laity, and to a lesser degree for administrators, parents of senior students, younger laity, and Lutheran faculty. Other groups seem quite satisfied with the colleges' efforts, especially college freshmen.

Earlier in this chapter, reference was made to certain specific expectations of students and faculty with respect to the stance of the college toward the Christian faith of students. It may now be appropriate to examine the manner in which these groups see their colleges fulfilling their expectations. Not only do more than one-half of the faculty members, Lutheran and non-Lutheran, support the expectation that their college should provide opportunities for growth in the Christian faith, but 44 percent agree that the college does "very well" or "quite well" in fulfilling the goal. An additional 36 percent say "somewhat well." Only 1 out of 10 says the college does "very little" in this respect, and only 17 out of 507 faculty responding say the college does it "not at all."

A Study of Generations, carried out among Lutherans ages fifteen to sixty-five, documents that most students, whether in church-related colleges or elsewhere, generally evidence a decline in religious activity during their college years.[4] Nevertheless, both freshman and senior respondents in LCA colleges not only apparently feel it is appropriate for their college to provide opportunities for growth in the Christian faith, but a significant percentage of them indicate that their college is actually doing so. When almost 80 percent of graduating seniors make such an affirmation concerning their college, and only 13 percent feel that the college has achieved this goal "very little" or "not at all," these students are also giving strong support to the claims of their colleges to be distinctively church-related institutions.

Nevertheless, just as most colleges are not satisfied to have won half of their football games, it is likely that few administrators will be satisfied with 44 percent of their students giving their religious program a good evaluation. Some college presidents viewing the 1960s and early 1970s in retrospect feel they were somewhat apologetic about this aspect of college life and therefore less aggressive in seeking this goal.

SOCIAL CHANGE

A fifth goal expectation is that the church-related college should contribute to the solution of social ills by equipping individuals of all ages with the necessary skills for working toward constructive changes in society. Six out of ten persons in the total sample judge it as "absolutely essential" or "very desirable" that the college contribute to the solution of community problems by creating a concern for human welfare, preparing students to bring about constructive social change, and assisting congregations in meeting social issues.

The expectation that a church-related college demonstrate community involvement for the purpose of effective social change has no doubt increased with the heightened social consciousness of recent years. That such an expectation appears among the six goals identified by LCA constituents is itself witness to a major change in both college and church communities.

Contributing to the solution of social ills does not mean, however, that the college should subordinate its major task of being an educational institution to that of serving as a social agency. Of all respondents, 80 percent express emphatic agreement with the statement "A college should not be viewed as a social tool to solve the pressing problems of church or society, but rather as an agency to educate persons who can later solve problems."

Responses tend to endorse the Partnership Statement of the LCA, which affirms the responsibility of all Christians to work with all people of goodwill for the enhancement of the quality of life enjoyed by the human family. The church looks to the colleges as partners in producing men and women who are equipped and motivated to be responsible citizens in the occupations and professions necessary to society's well-being. This role expectation of the church-related college is clearly shared by the overwhelming majority of college constituents.

With respect to the fulfillment of their expected role as educators and catalysts for social change, the colleges do not receive high marks from any of their constituents. College seniors express strongest disappointment, sharing an unusual alliance with faculty, LCA pastors, synod boards, and, to a lesser degree, college administrators.

In view of the common desire expressed by both college and church groups for a more effective role for the colleges in education on social issues, cooperative efforts by colleges and synods should be undertaken to strengthen this dimension of the colleges' programs. Social statements of the LCA, notably recent ones on human rights and on aging, provide basic resource material for study and action. Energies of interested students and expertise of college faculties are assets which can be employed fruitfully in fulfilling the social responsibilities of both partners.

RELIGIOUS DIVERSITY

A climate of religious diversity within a Christian orientation as a goal for LCA colleges appears to have gained least general acceptance among the constituent groups. While no one advocates a narrow parochialism, there still appears to be concern that the Christian faith may be regarded as simply another "cafeteria option" in the life of the college. This tension appears in the fact that while 65 percent of the entire constituency feel that it is "absolutely essential" or "very desirable" to provide an atmosphere of intellectual freedom, almost the same proportion, 68 percent, feel that most faculty in a church-related college should be professing Christians.

The responses of college and church leadership on the issue of religious diversity suggest that the differences which appear between these groups are differences in emphasis rather than basic disagreements concerning the desired character of the college. Pastors, synod boards, and laity show some reluctance to encourage religious pluralism as a college goal. Eighty-eight percent of the clergy agree that most faculty should be committed Christians. College administrators and faculty are most supportive of religious diversity as a goal, and they reflect considerable dissatisfaction over the degree in which it is being achieved. They are joined by students and younger laity, who are eager to avoid parochialism and to maintain an atmosphere of intellectual freedom. At the same time, responses on other scales indicate that most of these on-campus people do not wish to diminish the vitality of the Christian witness within their community.

On the other hand, the apparent lack of enthusiasm for greater diversity displayed by LCA pastors, laity, synod boards, and Lutheran alumni should not be seen as a mark of narrow parochialism. Their responses on other scales indicate strong support for interfaith dialogue and academic freedom. What they are expressing is their very real desire for a stronger Christian presence in both faculties and student bodies than is presently perceived.

SUMMARY

In summary, the constituents of LCA colleges expect their colleges to be first of all educational institutions of integrity, intent on providing students with an education which will develop their highest potential as human persons. While they are eager that professional competence be achieved, they value the human qualities of sensitivity, compassion, discriminating judgment, and moral responsibility more highly than job training. Their colleges are expected to provide climate and personnel which affirm the Christian faith and encourage the growth of students in that faith, while also supporting dialogue between Christian theology and other academic disciplines. They have clearly identified the six goals which have been examined in this chapter as normative for their institutions, and they have made realistic assessments of the extent to which these goals are being achieved.

Colleges of the LCA which purposefully affirm and actively seek to fulfill these goals may confidently claim their constituents' support as they move into the 1980s. In this pursuit they will join other church-related institutions in contributing a dimension to American higher education which educational institutions in the public sector are neither able nor constitutionally authorized to provide.

The independent, church-related college is able to base its educational program on Christian theological foundations, and its concern for every student upon an understanding of the human person as God's creation, and at the same time to proclaim the essential principle of diversity in the American system of higher education. The constituencies of LCA colleges have given resounding affirmation to such intents and goals. Faithfulness in their fulfillment by college leadership will provide a sound basis for the distinctiveness of the church-related colleges, and may well assure their significant survival in the waning years of the twentieth century.

3
Who Is in Charge?

During the late 1960s and early 1970s, one of the questions most frequently being asked of universities and colleges by the American public was, Who is in charge? No doubt there were more fundamental questions than this that needed desperately to be asked. One of these would relate to the goals and purposes of the mammoth educational structure which had been created in this country following World War II. But anyone who ventured into the quadrangle of Columbia University on September 10, 1968, and watched the angry crowds of students assault and occupy the offices of the university president, bringing the academic operation of that great institution to a halt, would surely raise the question of authority first.

The epidemic character of such occurrences on university and college campuses all across the country had the net effect of drawing public concern to more basic issues such as the purpose and goals of American education. But the question of the moment, born of panic and anger was, Who is in charge? Though scenes such as that at Columbia suggested that no one was really in charge, it was quite clear that both the insurgent students and the panicked public saw the president of the institution as the power center of the university.

This chapter will examine the question that hovered so disconcertingly over the campuses of all colleges during the embattled 1960s. Because our survey was conducted in the fall of 1975, the question was considered in a climate less highly charged with emotion. Responses were requested which probed for thoughtful expectations of college leadership. In the changed atmosphere, it became possible to measure perceptions of success not simply in terms of preventing the physical destruction of the college but in terms of achieving positive educational goals.

When respondents were asked for their expectations and perceptions of college administrators, it is likely that they, too, were thinking of the college president as "the man in charge." This person, rather than the group of colleagues and advisers who assist him with administrative duties, is the one often seen as "the administration." This tendency to personalize the administration must be kept in mind when interpreting the survey data about administrators.

COLLEGE ADMINISTRATORS

The administrative leaders participating in the survey were the president, academic dean, dean of students, director of development, finance officer, and chaplain of each college. Up to nine additional administrators also were included from each college, particularly those who help shape policy. Of the 189 administrators who participated in the survey, 63 percent are Lutheran, 60 percent of them belonging to the LCA. A total of 35 percent hold doctorates and 37 percent have earned master's degrees; 97 percent regard themselves as "moderately" or "deeply religious"; and 81 percent express their religious commitment as members of a congregation.

Competence and Caring

The first expectation, that administrators be competent and caring individuals, is accorded an importance exceeded only by one other grouping of items in the entire study, namely, "Competence of Faculty as Teachers."

A casual reading of the items included in this catalog of expectations leads one to agree with the whimsical judgment of a retired college president as he reflected on the qualifications prepared for the guidance of a presidential search committee. "In order to qualify for this position," he declared, "a person must combine the virtues and wisdom of Socrates, Solomon, St. Paul, and the Lord himself."

Not only is the list itself impressive, but the unusually high ratings given by respondents make it clear that the constituents of LCA colleges take these expectations seriously. Highest on the list are the expectations that Lutheran college administrators should show that they care about students and that they communicate well with the faculty. Ninety-two percent of all respondents list these two qualities as "absolutely essential" or "very desirable." Qualities such as compassion, availability, respect, vision, and the ability to articulate the college's mission are applauded by nearly 90 percent of the respondents. Expertise in college administration, faculty recruitment, and fund-raising likewise are highly rated.

Among the universally high ratings given these expectations, there is some variance among groups. Administrators give the highest importance of any group to these expectations of themselves. For example, the 72 percent of administrators according strong endorsement to the selection of qualified minorities for the faculty is well in advance of any other group. In like fashion, trustees and faculty show that they expect great things from their presidents and deans. The groups giving lowest ratings of importance are congregational laity of all ages.

In the judgment of most constituency groups, college administrators measure up quite well to these high expectations. Faculty members and senior students, however, register the widest spread between their expectations and their perceptions, and this is with respect to the qualities of administrative competence and caring.

Religious Commitment

LCA constituents also look for religious commitment in the administrators of their colleges. Such commitment is evidenced by active participation of such college officers in their church, as well as advocacy and interpretation of the Christian faith. While these qualities are clearly cherished by most respondents, the level of importance is not as high as on the previous scale, where only two of seventeen items show less than 72 percent strong endorsement. Of nine items dealing with religious commitment, the highest response of 75 percent was given to the effort of striving to preserve both the integrity of the college and its church relationship.

Some reticence is shown in expecting administrators to bear witness to their personal faith. Apparently they are viewed more as institutional agents, supporting the structures of faith and religion, than as individual witnessing members of the Christian community.

As might be surmised, the groups most sensitive to the religious orientation of college leaders and their efforts to strengthen college-church relationships are synod board members, LCA pastors, and trustees. Administrators and Lutheran faculty also place high value upon these efforts. Among students and non-Lutheran faculty, there is a striking mixture of responses. Some are strongly supportive, while a significant number feel the matter of an administrator's religious commitment to be of little importance.

It should be a matter of concern to the leadership of LCA colleges that the group registering the largest disparity between expectations and perceptions of the religious commitment of college administrators are clergy, synod boards, and all groups of congregational laity. The disappointment of clergy may be partially attributed to their extremely high expectations. But the negative response of the laity, who seem quite satisfied with the performance of college administrators as competent and caring persons, should occasion some careful self-examination by college officials. This is particularly so since college administrators, next to trustees, are the group which feels most strongly that a church-related college is an important part of the church's mission. Apparently, administrators need to find more effective ways to make this clear to members of congregations.

Views of College Administrators

In assessing the leadership of the colleges, it is important to know not only the expectations and perceptions of constituents but also the actual views of college administrators with respect to the goals of the college and the importance they accord a church relationship. How they understand institutional goals and how they rate their importance strongly influence the character and direction of the college.

Administrators of LCA colleges join the entire sample in placing highest value upon goals that contribute to "Wholeness of Person." The 86 percent that rate these goals as "absolutely essential" or "very desirable" is even stronger than the 78 percent endorsement by the total sample. Concern for student self-understanding and the development of a student's full potential within a community of caring people are their ideals for LCA institutions.

Of equal importance for administrators are the qualitative educational goals associated with the liberal arts. Education of the mind and the development of competent leaders to serve society also find strong expression in their responses to the "Preparation for Life" scale.

Though religious diversity among faculty and students is not widely appreciated by the general constituency, college administrators give it a strong endorsement. Almost 70 percent view such diversity as "absolutely essential" or "very desirable," and 85 percent place similar value upon the provision of an atmosphere of intellectual freedom, where the Christian faith is considered in dialogue with other beliefs.

With respect to the scale assessing the importance of a "Christian Perspective," administrators' scores equal those of the general constituency. Among on-campus groups, their expectations are the highest. They give strongest emphasis to providing quality education within a Christian perspective. Eighty-seven percent regard this as "absolutely essential" or "very desirable"; 78 percent feel it equally important to provide opportunity for growth in the Christian faith. Of least importance to administrators, as to most other groups, is the preparation of students for church occupations or for leadership in congregations. It seems quite clear that LCA colleges are no longer valued primarily as producers of clergy and other church workers. Their preferred role is to prepare persons for responsible citizenship and for service in a variety of professions. This concept of mission finds its impulse and rationale in the Lutheran understanding of Christian vocation.

It is clear that LCA college administrators place greatest value upon institutional goals which relate to the educative process and which are essentially student-centered. They want this process to be conducted in a climate conducive to Christian growth which is open to a variety of religious expressions.

One may wonder how this leadership stance compares with that of other church-related colleges. Fortunately, such a comparison is possible through a survey conducted at the National Congress of Church-Related Colleges and Universities at Notre Dame University in June 1979. More than 400 of the 700 delegates responded to a questionnaire embodying the thirty-six goal statements drawn from the *Research Report, A Survey of Images and Expectations of LCA Colleges.* Among these were 182 administrators, whose responses can be compared with those of the 189 LCA college administrators who participated in the LCA survey.[1]

Both similarities and differences appear in their responses to four comparable goal scales. Full concurrence was registered on the goal "Wholeness of Person." The LCA administrators and their ecumenical counterparts both assign it the highest importance. A notable difference appears in the importance accorded a liberal arts education, with 51 percent of the LCA group and only 35 percent of the ecumenical group rating it as "absolutely essential." Almost the reverse is true of the scale on "Christian Perspective," where 52 percent of the ecumenical group give it a rating of "absolutely essential," while only 39 percent of LCA leadership assign it this high value.

Items relating directly to social change are much less strongly supported by all administrators, although those of the LCA show considerably greater interest than their ecumenical colleagues. Thirty-one percent of the LCA group, but only 24 percent of the other group, feel it "absolutely essential" that the colleges provide the understanding and skills needed in working for constructive changes in society.

Religious diversity is also valued more highly by the LCA leadership, 48 percent feeling that it is "absolutely essential" to provide an atmosphere of intellectual freedom, where the Christian faith is considered in dialogue with other beliefs.

Both the LCA and Notre Dame surveys make it clear that administrators of church-related colleges share high aspirations for their institutions, educationally and with respect to a church relationship. However, in their very modest assessments of how these goals are actually being achieved, they also display a realistic understanding of the difficult tasks they and their institutions are facing.

BOARDS OF TRUSTEES

To discuss the issue "Who is in charge?" one should properly include the expectations and perceptions of college trustees, until recently the "sleeping giants" of college governance. Although boards of trustees have always been the final governing authority of most colleges and universities, vested by law with corporate responsibility for the affairs of the institution, their role has generally been overshadowed by administrators. As policymakers and monitors of the long-range welfare of the college, the board of trustees ought actually to give the definitive answer to the question, Who is in charge?

Of the 308 LCA college trustees who responded to the survey, 78 percent are Lutheran; one-third have annual incomes in excess of $40,000; and 60 percent hold master's or doctor's degrees. Nine out of ten consider themselves either "deeply" or "moderately religious" and are associated with an organized congregation.

A heightened sensitivity to the importance of their corporate and fiduciary responsibilities has led to widespread attention being given to a fuller understanding of trusteeship. In light of this development, it is instructive to note some of the self-perceptions of LCA college board members.

Four Concerns

First, they are virtually unanimous in recognizing their responsibility as policymakers. However, more than one-third of them feel that they are not carrying out this responsibility effectively. This may be why an overwhelming number (87 percent) underscores as "absolutely essential" or "very desirable" a careful nominating process when synods of the LCA select trustees. Only if this is done will able and dedicated persons be placed on the governing boards of the colleges. A comparatively meager 47 percent of the trustees venture the opinion that their synods are achieving this goal of careful selection "very well" or "quite well." Twelve percent indicate that they don't know what procedures are used. A 40 percent difference between the "should" and "is" of trustee selection suggests the need for careful review of synodical nominating procedures. Many synods operate without specially designed criteria for choosing nominees for their college boards. The stakes are far too high to risk the future of multi-million-dollar institutions for the sake of geographical representation, personal honor, or recognition.

A second concern centers in their understanding of the problems and potentials of their college. Although 86 percent of the trustees see this as a highly desirable function and responsibility, only 52 percent feel that they as trustees do a good job of reflecting such an understanding. A 34 percent discrepancy indicates the awareness of many trustees that they lack an understanding of basic problems and potentials of a church-related college. This deficiency could be remedied easily by a board-initiated program of orientation and education in the trusteeship of the church-related college.

A third area of concern relates to the task of communication. It is one trustees rate as being very important, but it is also one in which they feel inadequate. Although 67 percent deem it "very desirable" that they be involved in interpreting the college to their church constituencies, only 23 percent feel they are doing this even "quite well." Ten percent do not know whether it is being done at all.

A fourth issue relates to another task both trustees and synod board members view as highly important. It is the trustees' responsibility for communicating the church's concerns to the college. Here again, a disparity of 45 percent appears between the expectations and perceptions of both groups. More important is the fact that 51 percent of the trustees and 22 percent of the synod board members were unable to give an informed response and therefore chose a "don't know" answer regarding their perceptions.

During the past ten years, college boards of trustees have undertaken a variety of methods, often in response to heavy pressures, to open lines of communication with students and faculty. Luncheons and social hours have been held with students and faculty during board meetings; open forums for questions and answers have been conducted; and, in many instances, faculty and student representation at board or board committee meetings have been authorized. Trustees who responded to the survey apparently are not satisfied that these procedures have adequately achieved their intended purpose. Faculty and students agree. While a more energetic pursuit of this goal may be desired on the part of some boards, the achievement of general satisfaction seems quite unlikely. There will always be an aura of mystery about the role of a governing board, and on occasion a curtain of privacy will be drawn in the best interests of persons and of the institution. On the other hand, a board of trustees will be able to create a climate of confidence among its constituents by a prompt and open sharing of information on decisions that do not bear the stamp of confidentiality.

The trustees of LCA colleges place very high priority upon the issue of effecting closer college-church relationships, and a substantial majority feel that it is being treated as a vital concern. Most would welcome even more concerted efforts to bring together representative members of the faculties and the church to discuss ways of strengthening these ties. One significant effort in this direction has been a series of regional conferences on church-related higher education sponsored by the Department for Higher Education of the Division for Mission in North America. These conferences have assembled selected representatives of all the constituency groups included in the Survey of Images and Expectations. Trustees, faculty, pastors, students, and others have gathered for discussion of the LCA Partnership Statement and the survey report itself.

An Undeveloped Resource

There is obviously a vast and willing resource in the boards of trustees for improved college-church relations, a resource thus far largely undeveloped. No other constituency group reflects as strongly loyal support of their colleges as do the trustees, not even the presidents and their staffs.

Of all groups, trustees are among the most eager for a religiously distinctive college. They especially want theological engagement and education for moral responsibility to be taken seriously. Their support of religious diversity, as opposed to parochialism, is exceeded only by faculty and administration. They are strong advocates of the liberal arts. In agreement with the college faculties, they see the development of leadership qualities and intellectual acumen in students, rather than job training, as the best preparation for life. They do not look for the college to serve as an agency for social change. Their expectations in this regard are lower than among all groups except parents of freshman students and laity between the ages of thirty-six and fifty-one.

Generally speaking, the trustees tend to be rather uncritical of their school. Among all groups, they are generally among the last to believe negative reports about the college, its faculty, or its programs. By far the dominant opinion among them is that there is no significant drift away from the church on the part of their colleges.

Their eagerness to believe the best and their reluctance to give credence to situations which campus administrators view as problems may on occasion actually hinder effective policymaking. Trustees, for example, rate the sense of community on campus well above administrators and tend, like parents of freshmen, to see the campus as an integrated, caring community. Not only do they tend to minimize problems, but they also tend to overestimate positive results. Their perceptions of how well their college is educating for moral responsibility, for example, are well above those of all other constituency groups.

During the past few years, several trustee boards of LCA colleges have undertaken organized programs to improve the effectiveness of their operation. The Department for Higher Education of DMNA, together with the Aid Association for Lutherans, has helped in planning and financing trusteeship seminars at Lenoir-Rhyne College and California Lutheran College. Presidents and board chairmen of all LCA colleges have met as a group to discuss common concerns. Several LCA colleges have conducted board retreats or sponsored other activities that have a similar purpose.

One result of these seminars is that board members come to know not only each other and their college personnel but also the problems of the institution they serve and govern. At these seminars, board procedures have been studied and revised, and orientation sessions for new members have been introduced. Issue-oriented sessions, unencumbered by regular business agenda items, have been fitted into meeting schedules or arranged at other times and places. A fuller understanding of such matters as faculty tenure, student housing, financial aid, church relations, and investment policies has occurred. Long-range planning has been implemented, and in many instances a new sense of community has been established among trustees and their campus colleagues.

Other agencies also have undertaken major programs for the development of more effective trusteeship. An early contributor to this movement was Ralph Greenleaf, whose thoughtful booklets on "servanthood" in relation to institutions, trustees, and administrators have stimulated boards of trustees in industry and education to reexamine their functions and motivations.[2] The Association of Governing Boards of Universities and Colleges regularly publishes materials on trusteeship and sponsors an annual meeting for trustees of member institutions. It has greatly expanded its services in recent years, making available advisory services through a "Mentor Program" and a variety of other programs. The increased amount of litigation involving institutions of higher education has made boards of trustees more sensitive to issues of corporate liability. This has given rise to such organizations as the Center for Constitutional Studies at Notre Dame University, which offers legal counsel to educational institutions and their boards.

SUMMARY

It is impossible to overestimate the significance of the role played by trustees and administrators in shaping the stance and direction of educational institutions. Even with a competent and dedicated faculty, it is possible for an institution to fail in its mission (and probably lose its best faculty in the process) because it lacks a leadership that is purposeful and decisive.

This is especially true of small, church-related colleges, where the role of the president is highly visible and impinges on almost every phase of the college's life. The vitality of a church relationship will without question diminish or flourish in direct relationship to the attitudes of the president and the board of trustees. It is therefore essential that this concern be taken seriously by presidential search committees and the boards who elect the president. It is of equal importance for synods to employ a careful process of nominating and electing college trustees.

4
What Are the Teachers Like?

The value and effectiveness of the educational program of any college depend upon what happens in the classroom, laboratory, and library. Buildings, campuses, landscapes, friendly people, campus life, high ideals—even a vital chapel and religious-life program—will not, in the long run, achieve the real mission of the church in higher education unless there is a competent, sensitive, and committed faculty.

No doubt the greatest single asset of church-related colleges down through the years has been their corps of dedicated and competent teachers, many of whom have devoted an entire lifetime of service to a single institution. Before the days of endowments, federally financed buildings, and subsidized tuition, these scholars were instructing and inspiring students, sharing knowledge, wisdom, and example. By their frugality they made a financial as well as an academic contribution to the building of a sound tradition of liberal learning, grounded in a concern for humane values and the Christian faith.

Among older graduates of church-related colleges, almost every one can name one or two such professors whose example or precept exerted a significant influence in shaping their values or influencing their life choices. Our survey makes it clear that much of this same expectation of faculty persists to this day in the minds of LCA college constituents. The discrepancy between their expectations and perceptions is to some extent a measure of the degree to which church-related colleges have bowed to the demands of mass education in the hiring and retaining of teachers.

A brief overview of LCA college faculties in the fall of 1979 indicates a teaching corps numbering 1,492 persons, about 35 percent of whom are Lutheran. Seventy-six percent are male. Of the full-time faculty, 2.2 percent (33) are members of minority groups: blacks, Asians, or Hispanics. Sixty percent hold earned doctorates; 27 percent carry the rank of professor; 31 percent, associate professor; 30

48

percent, assistant professor; and 11 percent, instructor. The average student-faculty ratio for all colleges is 14.8 : 1.

The size of faculties in LCA colleges ranges from 15 to 142, with an average of 83. At four institutions the number exceeds 100.

Tenured faculty range from 43 percent to 82 percent, with the highest concentrations in the upper ranks. In ten of the eighteen schools, all persons with rank of full professor are permanently tenured, and in three, all persons at the rank of associate professor.

Levels of compensation in relation to rank vary greatly. Total compensation (salary and benefits) for full professors in 1979–80 averages $27,113; for associate professors, $21,712; for assistant professors, $18,075; and for instructors, $15,061. Several colleges rank above the 80th percentile of private church-related colleges, according to the annual salary scales published by the American Association of University Professors. Others, depending on location and resources, are in the lower brackets. Annual salary increases for all LCA colleges between 1971 and 1978 averaged 5.3 percent annually, in comparison with an average of 5.4 percent for all colleges in the United States. During the same span of years, the National Consumer Price Index rose an average of 7.6 percent each year.[1]

Data such as these may not be meaningful to many members of a college's constituency. With the possible exception of the percentage of doctorates on the faculty, neither students nor parents are likely to inquire about or be influenced by such information when making judgments about a college. But the attitudes and the performance of some members of the faculty are frequently determined by college policies and practices relating to each of these factors.

THREE EXPECTATIONS OF FACULTY

From the responses of all groups of constituents, three basic characteristics surface as most important for faculty members in LCA colleges. In order of importance, these are: (1) Competence as Teachers, (2) Commitment to Educational Mission, and (3) Christian Commitment.[2]

Competence as Teachers

The overwhelming selection of competence as the primary expectation of faculty members shows that constituencies of LCA colleges view their colleges first and foremost as educational institutions. There is no inclination to condone mediocrity in the classroom or to accept piety as a substitute for competence. Persons engaged to serve on their faculties are judged first of all on what they know and how well they communicate it to students. Such an expectation affirms the position of the LCA in its Partnership Statement, which asserts the integrity of the college's primary role as being that of a teaching institution.

The items that describe this expectation provide a profile of an ideal liberal arts college professor, an ideal to which few faculty members would take exception. Most important of all specific expectations is the ability of a teacher to awaken students' intellectual involvement in a subject. This quality in an LCA college professor is regarded as "absolutely essential" or "very desirable" by 93 percent of all respondents. No single expectation in any category receives a higher rating than this. Of primary importance is the expectation that able scholarship go hand in hand with competent teaching. All constituents, whether pastors, students, or professional colleagues, expect teachers to set a worthy example for their students. High tribute is paid to the quality of sensitivity which, realizing the gap between the professor's educational level and that of students, seeks without arrogance or condescension to encourage intellectual growth and maturity.

Part of a student's quest in these growing years is the search for meaning in all of life. In a college which views this quest as central to the educational process, the readiness of a faculty member to reach out to students is an essential quality.

Professional parochialism has no place in the expectations of a faculty. On the contrary, good teachers awaken in students an awareness of how their discipline relates to other fields of knowledge. They demonstrate respect and appreciation for the contributions of other faculty members, and they deal tolerantly with points of view other than their own. They reflect a humane concern for all people. Even in a time when professorial loyalties tend to focus primarily on one's own discipline and one's personal professional status, a sense of pride in one's college is an important expectation of 86 percent of the total constituency.

Significantly, the highest expectations of college faculty bear a close resemblance to the institutional goals most desired by constituencies. The specific components of these general goals of "Wholeness of Person" and "Preparation for Life" were education of the mind; gaining self-understanding; integrating intellectual knowledge, ethical sensitivity, and concrete action; gaining a positive attitude toward life-long learning; fulfilling potentials and accepting limitations; and gaining mastery of some specific field of knowledge.

While not the exclusive responsibility of the faculty, these components directly involve the relationship of student with professor. In the eyes of most respondents, faculty are seen as ultimately responsible for the success or failure of a college to achieve its most important goals. Without detracting from the important roles of college president, dean, counselor, or chaplain, this view speaks well for the educational understanding of the constituencies of LCA colleges.

Matching the almost universal agreement of the high importance of teaching competence is the quite general satisfaction with the level of faculty performance. In the judgment of most college constituencies, faculty in LCA colleges are competent teachers. Parents, especially freshman parents, indicate strongest commendation. Pastors, trustees, alumni, and congregational laity likewise have no hesitation about the quality of teaching.

Another assessment of faculty competence is supplied by items which evaluate the general quality of education provided by a college. Responses to these items also reveal an image of competent and demanding faculty who provide student-centered instruction of high quality. Well over one-half the total sample agree that their college offers a superior quality of education—the kind that makes parents willing to borrow, if necessary, to send their children. Parents of freshman and senior students, who actually do the borrowing, indicate nearly 70 percent agreement with this evaluation of their college. Almost as notable is the fact that only one in ten senior students registers any negative judgment, while 60 percent of them affirm the assessment, describing their college as academically "tough" or demanding.

The groups least ready to award high grades to faculty are the faculty themselves, administrators, and senior students. The limited commendation of these latter two groups, one professionally responsible for performance evaluation and the other the most directly involved "consumer," suggests the improvement of teaching attitudes and teaching techniques as a worthy area for faculty development programs.

Some recognition of this need on the part of faculty members themselves may be inferred from their own reluctance to indulge in self-approbation. They, as much as most, feel they do not meet fully such subjective expectations as "bridging the gap between their own intellectual level and that of the students." The increasing faculty endorsement and use of various devices such as student questionnaires for evaluating their classroom competence provides additional evidence of faculty concern for self-improvement.

Commitment to Educational Mission

The second-ranking expectation of college faculty is their visible commitment to the educational mission of the college. Respondents in general make a distinction between academic teaching and professional activities outside the classroom, such as establishing close relationships with students and pursuing individual programs of scholarly research. Other related activities include participating with faculty colleagues in constructive dialogue on issues of faith, philosophy, or ethics, and sharing expertise with community leaders outside the classroom, thereby demonstrating a concern for the quality of community life. A readiness to enter into such activities is viewed as evidence of a commitment to the educational mission of a church-related college.

Sixty percent of the total sample regard such activities as "absolutely essential" or "very desirable," with very little divergence of opinion among the various groups of respondents. Personal attention to students and engagement in scholarly activity or research are the two evidences of faculty commitment to an educational mission valued most.

Fewer of the respondents are ready to affirm that expectations related to this mission are being met "very well" or "quite well." The largest numbers of those who are in a position to know of the extracurricular activities of faculty, such as administrators, trustees, and faculty members themselves, prefer to say their expectations are being "somewhat" fulfilled. It is also quite clear that large percentages of such off-campus groups as pastors, synod board members, laity, parents, and even alumni do not know of the ways in which faculty members make their professional expertise available in their local communities or in larger circles. To give greater visibility to these activities would enhance the image of the college and its faculty as being people-oriented, scholarly, and concerned about their wider community.

LCA college faculty, however, have been quite successful in establishing personal relationships with their students. Only 8 percent of the students indicate that faculty have done little or nothing to fulfill this expectation of close student-faculty relationships. Sixty-seven percent of the freshmen and 52 percent of the seniors feel their faculty have done "very well" or "quite well" in learning to know many students personally.

In the interest of fairness, the survey instrument included several items which reflect the kind of caustic negative criticism of a college and its faculty occasionally voiced on or off campus. These items were based on actual quotations given in interviews on LCA college campuses when the content of the entire questionnaire was being determined. They describe faculty who evidence divisive attitudes, lack of commitment to the mission of the college, complacency, intellectual snobbery, disinterest in students, and lack of academic rigor.

Few people, about one in ten, attribute such characteristics to LCA college faculties, though admittedly most faculties can name persons who not only fail to make positive contributions to the broader educational mission of the college but on occasion hinder it.

Christian Commitment

While it is quite clear that college constituencies expect a high degree of religious sensitivity from their faculty, it is not expected that this sensitivity be expressed according to any uniform pattern. The reason resides in the fact that religious diversity is a goal of the same constituency.

The variety and breadth of this diversity is reflected in the following items which were associated in survey responses with the concept of Christian commitment. These quite diverse activities are generally

seen as expressions of Christian commitment on a college campus
and for that reason intercorrelated to form the cluster.

- Support visibly the religious program of the college
- See themselves as shaping a college which is distinctively church-
  related
- Participate actively with a local congregation
- Understand and appreciate Lutheran theology and tradition
- Provide examples of people who combine a keen intellect with a
  Christian faith
- Recognize that the subject of faith is appropriate for all parts of
  the college
- Show concern for the moral and spiritual development of their
  students, as well as their intellectual growth

A large majority, 78 percent of all respondents, want faculty to
show concern for the moral and spiritual development of their students, as well as their intellectual growth. More than half want faculty
to provide visible support for the religious program of the college,
to help shape the college as a distinctively church-related institution,
and to encourage discussions relating to religious faith. But fewer than
half regard it as "absolutely essential" that faculty be actively involved in a local congregation or that they understand and appreciate
Lutheran theology and tradition.

Variety appears also in the differing responses of constituent
groups. For example, the item on faculty understanding and appre-
ciating Lutheran theology is rated highly by two-thirds of Lutheran
clergy, with one-fourth of them rating it as "absolutely essential." In
contrast, 40 percent of the parents of freshman and senior students,
many of whom are non-Lutheran, view this evidence of religious commitment as of no importance or, at most, "somewhat desirable."

In like fashion, two-thirds of the pastors, but only one-third of the
faculty, regard activity within a local congregation as "absolutely
essential" or "very desirable." Differences within groups fade, however, when rating the importance of faculty engaging in sympathetic
and wise conversations with students suffering intellectual and spiritual distress. This less formal manifestation of religious sensitivity is
considered far more important than being active in one's local
congregation.

Issue of the "Critical Mass"

Whatever differences exist among individuals and groups regarding the hallmarks of Christian commitment, the basic question is posed by one specific item in the survey: How important is it that faculty of a church-related college include a significant number of committed Christians?

Lutheran colleges, which historically have maintained close denominational ties, must also ask themselves: How many faculty members ought to be Lutherans? Are there certain key positions in the faculty and administration which should be filled by Lutherans, for the college to remain effectively linked with the denomination? These questions pose the crucial issue of a "critical mass."

This concern is becoming increasingly important, especially in areas where the Lutheran constituency is small. Lutheran educators agree that a strong Lutheran representation is more important within faculty and administration than within student population. In 1979 the average enrollment of Lutheran students in all LCA colleges was 27 percent. In several institutions the percentage was less than 20 percent, and in two instances less than 10 percent. Eight LCA colleges enrolled more Roman Catholics than Lutherans.

As eager as the colleges and church are to serve larger numbers of Lutheran students, it is generally agreed that the identity of the institutions is essentially determined by the board of trustees, faculty, and administration. At the present time, 70 percent of the trustees and 35 percent of the faculties are Lutheran. Fifteen of the eighteen LCA college presidents are Lutheran.

The percentage of Lutheran faculty has declined in recent years; in some institutions it is as low as the percentage of Lutheran students. Moreover, faculty members display much stronger support for religious diversity in their college than does the average respondent. Therefore, the question of faculty attitude on the issue of critical mass is an important one.

No magic number or percentage can be given as to what constitutes the critical mass for Lutheran colleges, but for 68 percent of the total constituency it is clear that "*most* faculty at a church-related college should be professing Christians." Whether "most" implies a simple majority or a more substantial majority is impossible to determine. The fact, however, that 85 percent of trustees, pastors, and synod board members affirm the principle of a majority is significant. Tension over this issue is seen in the fact that less than half the non-Lutheran faculty and only 34 percent of the students concur. Clearly, two quite different points of view exist regarding the importance of maintaining a Christian perspective. And this difference centers not in maintaining a "Lutheran core" but more broadly in maintaining a significant core of professing Christians of all denominations.

FOUR PREDICTORS OF FACULTY SUPPORT

There is an analytical procedure made possible by computer analysis that isolates important variables in people's responses to items in the questionnaire.[3] Information secured by this means enables one to predict the kinds of responses that might be anticipated from certain groups of persons under certain identifiable conditions or circumstances. This analytic procedure helps answer an important question germane to a key issue of this chapter. Who among the faculty are most likely to support increased activity toward a colleague relationship with the church? Who are most likely to resist such a development?

Four predictors surface through the analysis as strong indicators of the faculty who are likely to give the strongest support for a close college-church relationship. In order of importance, the indicators are these: (1) declared religious commitment, (2) participating membership in an organized congregation, (3) area of residence, and (4) age. These four criteria predict whether there will be support or resistance from faculty in a college. Since religious commitment emerges as the most important predictor of the four, closer attention will be given this dimension of faculty life.

Religious Commitment

All persons surveyed were asked to describe their present religious commitment or orientation, using one of the following descriptions:
1. Deeply religious, within the framework of an organized religion
2. Deeply religious, outside the framework of an organized religion
3. Moderately religious, within the framework of an organized religion

4. Moderately religious, outside the framework of an organized religion
5. Largely indifferent to religion
6. Basically opposed to religion

Faculty responses provide an interesting point of comparison with the images they have established in the eyes of constituent groups. First of all, most of them are not Lutheran. Of the total randomized sample of all eighteen college faculties where an 80 percent response was received, no more than one-third of the 851 respondents are Lutheran. These two groups—Lutheran and non-Lutheran faculty— differ strikingly on how they view themselves religiously. Forty-three percent of the Lutheran faculty identify themselves as deeply religious, as compared with 26 percent of the non-Lutherans. Only 3 percent of the faculty Lutherans refer to themselves as indifferent or opposed to religion, whereas 15 percent of the non-Lutherans indicate personal indifference or opposition. Eighty-five percent of the Lutheran faculty members say they are participating members of congregations, while 47 percent of the non-Lutherans so respond.

If the percentages on religious indifference were extrapolated to embrace the total full-time faculties of the eighteen LCA colleges, there would be reason to be seriously concerned over the influence exerted by 263 faculty members, Lutheran or non-Lutheran, who identify themselves as being indifferent or opposed to religion. Granted, the presence of some non-Christians on college faculties provides a desirable opportunity for dialogue and intellectual growth. However, the presence of significant numbers of teachers who actually profess indifference to so fundamental a dimension of human culture as religion may constitute as much of a threat to liberal education as to Christian witness.

SUMMARY

It seems quite clear that among the constituencies of LCA colleges the role of the faculty is held in high esteem. The colleges are viewed primarily as teaching institutions, and the goals that constituents value most highly are those which are most dependent upon the competence of the faculty and its commitment to the development of students as whole persons.

Constituent groups express their expectations of faculty in three major categories: Competence as Teachers, Commitment to Educational Mission, and Christian Commitment. In their performance as teachers, rated by all groups as the most important criterion, faculty earn both respect and commendation. LCA college faculty are seen generally as competent scholars and able teachers who provide educational opportunities of high quality for their students. Somewhat less satisfaction is recorded for their involvement in professional and community activities outside the classroom. However, included in this category of expectations is the establishment of personal relationships with students. With respect to this aspect of their work, LCA college faculty are commended for their efforts by campus constituency groups, including the students themselves.

Expectations in the area of Christian commitment vary greatly, both as to definition and degree. A central concern is that of "the critical mass." Religious diversity is regarded as a desirable goal by the majority of constituents, but the question of how many persons with Christian commitment are needed on the faculty to maintain the vitality of the college's character as a church-related institution remains an issue causing real concern, especially among college leadership and the clergy.

One of the unfortunate legacies of the period of forced growth among LCA colleges, when teachers were scarce and enrollments exploding, is the cadre of faculty who were added without much inquiry as to their own religious commitment or the stated educational goals of the institutions. Many of these have since been "tenured in," and little can be done about it.

It is therefore of highest importance now, as vacancies and retirements occur, that most careful scrutiny be given not only to the academic credentials of faculty candidates but also to their sensitivity to the entire range of student needs—spiritual, social, and academic. Colleges related to the LCA should require of all faculty and administrators a commitment to goals which are both appropriate to an educational institution and compatible with the church's mission as an agency for service to the human family. Such a commitment may be expected of Christians or non-Christians, Lutherans or non-Lutherans. The future and character of all church-related colleges depend as much upon this selection process as upon funding and enrollments.

5

What Is Distinctive About Our Colleges?

In *The Responsible Campus* (1977) Charles McCoy[1] points to an "identity crisis" as one of the principal contemporary problems of church-related colleges. This crisis, according to Christopher Jencks and David Riesman (1968),[2] results from the efforts of many church-related colleges to cope with the academic revolution of the 1950s and 1960s by simply accepting the prevailing viewpoint of the academic profession about what, how, and when a college should teach. In seeking to emulate larger and often more prestigious public and private institutions, these church-related colleges have not only failed to gain the world but are in the process of losing their own souls.

This concern has been voiced also within the constituencies of the LCA colleges. They have watched as their colleges have grown, expanding and diversifying their faculties and student bodies to meet the enrollment demands of the public during the 1950s and 1960s. It has seemed, at least to some, that they are in danger of losing their character and becoming submerged in the gray sameness of the American academic scene.

Whether this is true or not, the question of distinctiveness, especially as expressed through the role of religion in the life of the campus, is important, both to the colleges and to their supporting churches.

There is a sense in which every college or university is different from all others. Each has a separate history, a specific geographical location, a particular group of persons serving as faculty and administrators. Each has its own name, its own students.

There is also a sense in which all academic institutions are alike. They are organized centers of learning, patterned to grant degrees in certain standard areas of study.

They may vary within descriptive categories as to size, quality, curriculum, or governance. But they are educational institutions, pursuing educational goals, whether sponsored by the state, the church, or a self-perpetuating board of trustees.

It should, of course, be apparent to any observer that institutional anonymity is a lurking danger for most colleges and universities in America, not alone for church-related colleges. Indeed, it may be expecting too much of 3,055 institutions of higher learning in this country that each should be significantly different, even from all others within its own category.

The category of church-related colleges, which includes 24 percent of all degree-granting institutions in the United States, is itself so broad and diverse that efforts to identify characteristics distinctive of all colleges in this category are not very useful. Even the term itself is difficult to define. As Cunninggim (1978)[3] observes, "A college is never absolutely, completely church-related. It is always less or more church-related than it was last year; than it intends to be next year; than its denomination thinks it is or wants it to be; than is some other college of its denomination; than are colleges connected with other denominations; etc., etc."

Nevertheless, Cunninggim himself has identified eight minimum essentials for church relatedness. "To be church-related, a college must 1) want to be; 2) make proper provision for religion in all its dimensions; 3) put its values and those of the church into recognizable operation; 4) be able to count on its church's understanding of the educational task; 5) receive tangible support from its church; 6) be made to feel that the denomination also gives it intangible support; 7) inform and illumine its denomination and welcome being informed and illumined in return; 8) know *why* it wants to be so related, and the church must know why *it* wants connections with its colleges."[4]

The degree to which colleges of any denomination meet even these minimum standards varies widely. Even within a denomination both images and expectations vary, as attested to by the survey upon which this book is based.

The Lutheran Church in America has identified a series of standards upon which it bases its official recognition of its related colleges. Published in 1970 in a brochure entitled "The Mission of LCA Colleges and Universities," these standards constitute the "distinctive qualities" of church relatedness.[5] They are:

1. *Affirmation of commitment.* The college's institutional goals shall reflect a commitment to Christian life and learning.
2. *Affirmation of church relationship.* The college shall affirm in its governing documents that a relationship exists with the Lutheran Church in America.
3. *Academic quality.* The college shall be accredited by the appropriate regional accrediting agency.
4. *Academic freedom.* The college shall maintain and uphold academic freedom for students, faculty, and administrators consistent with the 1940 statement of the American Association of University Professors.

As evidence of its commitment to Christian life and learning, the college is expected also to recruit faculty and students who respect its basic goals and commitments, including its relationship to the Lutheran Church in America. It is expected to provide regular opportunities for Christian worship as a part of the college program; a chaplain who is concerned primarily with worship and other dimensions of pastoral ministry in the life of the college; a competent program of courses in religion; opportunities for Christian service; and freedom for Christian witness by faculty, students, administrators. Further, the college is expected to be willing to serve as a resource for the church and to demonstrate a sense of social responsibility.

CAMPUS RELIGIOUS PROGRAMS

Many of these expectations are also emphasized by constituents of the LCA colleges in their identification of appropriate goals for the colleges. Specific attention focuses on the role and effectiveness of religious life as a distinctive feature of the church-related campus.

One scale measures constituents' expectations of the college's commitment to an active Christian ministry within the college community, as evidenced by activities, programs, and courses sponsored by the college. Among all respondents, six out of ten regard such a commitment as "absolutely essential" or "very desirable." These respondents want religious services which help students reexamine their commitment of faith, commemorate major Christian festivals, and transmit the heritage of the Christian church. They want the college to sponsor courses in the religious heritage and theology of the Lutheran tradition, religion courses which help students find a theological foundation for their faith, and activities which help students integrate their learning into a Christian perspective. They expect the college to provide a chaplain who ministers to the entire campus community, and above all, they want the Christian faith to be presented in a way that is intellectually respectable.

A list of expectations such as this might appear to be self-evident for any college that takes its church relationship seriously. Most colleges related to the LCA would affirm them as normal expressions of their religious commitment. It is actually surprising that as few as six out of ten respondents give them a high rating. Forty percent of the entire sample are at best lukewarm in their assessment of the importance of an organized religious life program on the campuses of church-related colleges.

A closer examination of the individual groups shows, as might be expected, strong general support among LCA clergy, synod board members, administrative leaders, and trustees. These groups are joined by Lutheran faculty and congregational laity, who feel strongly the importance of organized campus religious programs. But responses also indicate that one out of four members of the clergy do not regard campus religious services as useful means for helping students reexamine their commitments of faith. An even larger percentage is reluctant to commend the use of chapel services as a means of transmitting the heritage of the Christian church.

Showing least enthusiasm for campus religious programs are non-Lutheran faculty members. Only one-half of those responding regard such a religious emphasis as "absolutely essential" or "very desirable," and about one in five could dispense altogether with activities involving corporate worship, chapel services, and religion courses. Lutheran faculty, in contrast, are highly supportive of the campus religious programs.

Just a step above the non-Lutheran faculty are students. Whether freshmen or seniors, one-half express very little interest in organized campus religious programs. Apparently it makes little difference whether students are newcomers in college, transplanted directly out of communities and parishes, or whether they have been exposed to campus influences for three or four years. The college chaplain and the parish pastor seem to be waging the same difficult battle to capture the enthusiasm of younger people for conventional organized church activities.

On the other hand, quite favorable judgments are expressed concerning the actual quality of religious life on the campus. Well over half agree that the Christian gospel is being adequately proclaimed on the campus. Nearly 70 percent believe that most students respect the Christian orientation of the college, although less than half feel that most students are satisfied with the organized religious program. Two out of three agree that students who take a strong interest in religious activities can do so without being ridiculed or considered odd. Only 12 percent feel that the religious programs are exclusive and discourage broad participation, and only 5 percent feel that non-Lutherans on campus are given the uncomfortable feeling of being outsiders.

On the sensitive question of whether religion professors often undermine the faith of their students, only one out of seven believes that this is taking place. Almost half the total sample deny that this is the case, and one-third are unable to offer a judgment.

Although the total sample give quite favorable judgments on the quality of religious life in the colleges, there is no uniformity among the groups. Among campus groups, who could be expected to be more informed on these questions, faculty and administrators tend to agree with the general average. Senior students, however, express more negative feelings. Of the off-campus groups, parents, trustees and congregational laity, especially the older group, reflect more than average satisfaction. Pastors and synod board members register almost as strong a negative judgment as senior students.

Respondents to the survey also had opportunity to indicate their expectations of the college chaplain, especially as he functions in the role of pastor and personal counselor. Three out of four persons value his services as a guide for those searching for a personal faith, and 85 percent view the chaplain as someone with whom students could talk about almost anything. On the other hand, a reconciling ministry among faculty is regarded as important by less than half of all respondents, and by only two out of five faculty members. With the exception of the LCA clergy and senior students, most of the constituents in all groups are reasonably satisfied with the way personal ministry among students is being carried out on the college campuses.

RELIGION AS AN ACADEMIC DISCIPLINE

Another very specific question was posed by the survey. It asked: Is the religion department of the college regarded as among the best departments on campus? Responses indicate that such a reputation has not been established. Among the total sample, only 22 percent respond affirmatively, while 24 percent register negative judgments. Among the 38 percent unable to respond, a high percentage are congregational laity. It is not surprising that most of them do not feel sufficiently informed to venture a judgment.

On-campus groups, the ones who should be best able to judge, are more negative than affirmative. Lutheran faculty members and administrators respond most favorably, but their negative responses are exceeded only by senior students, 48 percent of whom decline to rank the religion department among the strongest departments in their college.

One may take issue with the way in which this question was posed, or with the basis on which judgments were made by different groups. Departmental strength no doubt also varies greatly among the eighteen colleges. Nevertheless, it seems fair to conclude that, in general, departments of religion in LCA colleges have yet to achieve an outstanding reputation.

The presence and vitality of theological dialogue is a much more sophisticated expectation than that of the frequency and visibility of chapel services or the availability of a chaplain on campus, or even the comparative reputation of religion departments. It deals with curriculum, campus conversation, and the ability and willingness of many persons to articulate the relationship between theology and other disciplines. Some degree of theological literacy on the part of all faculty and staff is requisite for effective fulfillment of this expectation.

Six out of ten respondents expect that students will be involved in thinking theologically about problems of human existence. They believe that religion instructors should engage students in wrestling with profound philosophical and religious questions, and that students should be encouraged to adopt Judeo-Christian values in making ethical decisions. They are most eager that the Christian faith be presented in a way that is intellectually respectable.

Which groups especially want this kind of theological engagement? Most eager are administrative leaders, Lutheran faculty, pastors, and trustees. Students, parents, and congregational laity see it as least important. Congregational laity actually place a lower value on such interaction than do parents of freshman and senior students.

Whether expectations are high or low, however, none of the groups perceives that theological engagement is being effectively carried out. More than half of the total sample and almost 70 percent of the laity indicate that they do not know how well this is being done. Among those who do venture a judgment, trustees, administrators, and Lutheran faculty are most satisfied. The low perceptions of pastors and synod board members stand in sharp contrast to their high expectations.

Of all the groups, the faculty itself should be most knowledgeable as to whether theological dialogue actually takes place between the various disciplines. Faculty responses to a group of items specifically addressed to this question indicate that in their judgment such dialogue is not being effectively carried out on their campuses. One out of four affirms that it is being handled "very well" or "quite well." A larger group, 40 percent, indicates that such discussions do occur "somewhat." One-fourth say "none" or "very little," and 10 percent say they do not know.

Senior students respond similarly to a series of questions dealing with the sensitivity of faculty members to students' search for meaning in life and their willingness to reach out to students rather than waiting for them to seek help. Almost 70 percent of senior students agree that theological engagements of this kind are taking place between faculty and students, but their modest ratings indicate that much more could be done. Only one in three feel this expectation is being fulfilled "very well" or "quite well." Even granting the difficulty of accurately assessing a characteristic of this kind, it is clear that much more effort on the part of the college leadership is needed if the expectations of constituents are to be met.

EDUCATION FOR VALUES AND
MORAL RESPONSIBILITY

Among the distinctive roles of the church-related college identified by the LCP Partnership Statement as especially important is that of fostering responsible citizenship. Citizenship in this context is broadly understood as the fulfillment of all of life's obligations, including those related to occupation or profession, in accord with high ethical standards and with a sense of interdependence and human compassion. This concern is seen to be of particular importance in a society that is divided and uncertain about its values and its future.

The survey sought to ascertain how widespread among college constituencies is this expectation that colleges affirm a value stance and education for moral responsibility, and to what degree campus life provides the setting which fosters responsible living and concern for others.

Further evidence on this important issue is drawn from constituency responses to a series of items dealing with questions of college policy and others describing student attitudes, interests and behaviors. High percentages of college constituencies want their college to have an impact on the moral and ethical lives of students. More than eight out of ten want the college to inform students as to what conduct is expected at the college and to use approaches that foster growth in a sense of moral responsibility, including resident living that develops an atmosphere of trust and caring. They believe the college should teach that respect for others is a basic principle on which conduct should be based. Seven out of ten believe that students should be helped to examine the relationship of personal values to societal values and should participate in making regulations and then be held accountable for carrying out their decisions, as well as learn to distinguish between legal, ethical, and moral issues. An equal number believe that student rights should be balanced with the right of a college to maintain a good public image, and that students should be challenged to adopt behaviors consistent with the ideals of the college.

Few clusters of items in the entire survey have elicited higher responses to every item in the cluster. An average of all responses indicates that three out of four persons endorse these aspects of education for moral responsibility.

The high correlation between responses on this scale and those on other scales measuring expectations of the colleges is most instructive. Correlational analyses indicate that persons who place a high value on education for moral responsibility also tend to favor close college-church relationships, a religious emphasis at their college, competent faculty, and competent, caring administrators who are religiously committed.

The groups giving highest importance to these educative efforts are trustees, administrative leaders of the college, and parents, with parents evidently more concerned over student manners and morals than over a campus religious climate. Though student ratings are the lowest of all groups, an average of well over 60 percent of students regard these expectations as "absolutely essential" or "very desirable."

It is an interesting phenomenon, and one which most deans of student affairs will recognize, that while students may express warm support for principles of social-community responsibility, they often tend to react protectively in relation to issues affecting their own personal freedom. One of the difficulties in assessing the status of real moral sensitivity among all groups, especially the younger ones, is the inherent resistance of some to accepting any presumably imposed definitions or standards of conduct, even those with which they may agree. As a case in point, in reacting to the assertion that their college should "convey the impression that students can do as they please," 46 percent of the freshmen and 39 percent of the seniors respond affirmatively.

In seeking to be fair in our judgments in this context, there is a danger of being overly optimistic, naively discounting the forces in our society which begin very early to instill in young people attitudes expressed in self-aggrandizement and vulgarity. Even if the colleges were more intent on moral education than they are, they would find it difficult to overcome the effects of eighteen years of youthful life in the decades of the 1960s and 1970s.

One of the most sobering insights of the entire survey comes in response to the item which stated: "The policy or approach of my college should be: to encourage students to adopt Judeo-Christian values in the treatment of others."

It would be difficult to see such a statement as a threat to anyone's personal independence. Yet only one-third of the freshmen, seniors, and younger laity regard the encouragement of Judeo-Christian values as "absolutely essential" or "very desirable" in the life of the college.

It is possible that this dismal student response rests upon an equally dismal religious illiteracy which does not know the meaning of the term "Judeo-Christian." Some support for this conclusion may be found in the fact that most of the older constituent groups—including parents, faculty, administrators, trustees, alumni, and pastors—apparently do understand its correlation with other items relating to moral education and rate it accordingly.

In view of the strong general endorsement of moral education as an important dimension of the program of the church-related college, it is also appropriate to inquire how well the constituent groups feel it is being fulfilled. Nearly all groups see the colleges doing a reasonably good job in moral education, though about 30 percent do not feel able to make a judgment. Yet only one student out of four believes that the college encourages students to adopt Judeo-Christian values.

Another very specific item calling for a value stance produced some surprising responses from LCA college constituents. This item stated: "The policy or approach of my college should be: to make it known that sexual intercourse between unmarried students is unacceptable."

Our analyses point out the interesting fact that this item correlates closely with thirty-four other items that reflect a religious emphasis, indicating that the issue involved is viewed as a part of the religious distinctiveness found at a college.

Contrasts in response to the item are striking. Seven out of ten parents and laity over fifty-two years of age believe the college should make it known that sexual intercourse between unmarried students is unacceptable. Six out of ten trustees, laity thirty-six to fifty-one years of age, LCA pastors, and synod board members agree. Only four out of ten administrators, alumni, and younger laity affirm such a policy. Even less support comes from Lutheran faculty and freshman students, and among non-Lutheran faculty and senior students, only two out of ten thought fornication should not be countenanced.

Clearly, least enthusiasm for calling sexual intercourse between unmarried students unacceptable is found among persons on campus —students, faculty, and administrators. Strongest support for such a policy comes from parents, church leaders, and church members. It may, however, come as a surprise to this latter group that as many as 35 percent of their number do not favor a strong college policy on extramarital sexual relations. Whatever the causes may be, it should be clear to both friends and critics of the colleges that standards of acceptable moral behavior have undergone significant change in recent years, among adults as well as young people. It may well be that both church and college will need to rethink their own roles in relation to standards of moral conduct and decide whether they are to be leaders or followers as they go about the task of teaching the young.

THE CAMPUS AS COMMUNITY

Another dimension of distinctiveness to which church-related colleges frequently lay claim is that of community spirit. Most church-related colleges are small in size and primarily residential in character. While these characteristics are not exclusively claimed by such colleges, they do lend themselves to the nurturing of qualities which the church-related colleges feel to be integral to the educational process. Experiences of common worship, social activities, and dormitory living have been seen as important in establishing the setting which would encourage personal integration and growth. Interaction between faculty and students has been seen as setting the moral tone and value orientation of the community and thus fostering a sense of moral responsibility. For these reasons the community life of the college has been considered an integral part of the educational program.

In the survey data a group of items formed a cluster focusing on the college as a community, reflecting feelings of acceptance and togetherness, involving students of diverse backgrounds, and assessing the college's concern for job placement and social service opportunities for students.

Senior students, those most conscious of how students generally feel about their college community, probably provide the most realistic response to this set of agree/disagree items. Community life, in their judgment, does exert an influence in the development of a sense of moral responsibility among students. Six out of ten seniors agree that "there are definitely 'unwritten rules' for behavior at this college —an expectation of how people should behave in moral matters."

Further, eight out of ten believe "the small size of a college gives each student a sense of accountability that comes from being well-known by peers."

Three out of four seniors agree that ample opportunity is given to students for involvement in social service activities. About half say that students on their campus associate with other students whose racial, ethnic, or social backgrounds are different from their own; one-third disagree with that statement. Less than one-third believe that minority students feel they are an integral part of the campus community or that their college does a good job of attracting minority students.

Community-related areas in which low ratings are given by students are job placement and preferential treatment of athletes. Only 25 percent feel they receive adequate help in finding jobs when they graduate, though the response might have been better if the seniors had been surveyed in June rather than early in their final year. Significantly, 56 percent feel that their college accords preferential treatment to athletes, a circumstance which they feel is not conducive to community building on the campus.

While these items are too few and too limited in scope to provide sufficient data for any conclusive judgment on community life, it is clear that one-third of senior students are conscious of specific factors which erode a sense of community, and another one-fourth are not clear about how to describe what is occurring. The positive response of only 43 percent of seniors suggests that much remains to be achieved in community building on LCA college campuses.

Another approach to the assessment of community atmosphere is provided by responses to a series of actual quotations from campus interviews in which conversations illustrated attitudes of divisiveness. Two items elicit fairly strong concurrence. Six out of ten seniors perceive that many students are more concerned about their social lives than about academic responsibilities. An equal proportion believes that black students at the college generally segregate themselves from other students. Two other items draw agreement from 40 percent of the seniors: that most students have little or no interest in critical campus issues and that students who attend their colleges are generally from homes of wealthy parents. However, an equal percentage of seniors disagree with these statements.

Disagreement is indicated with the remaining eight quotations describing antisocial attitudes. Six out of ten disagree with statements reflecting cutthroat competition, the need to cheat to stay competitive, or that emphasis placed on academic achievement leaves students with neither time nor energy to establish a caring community.

Generally, the other on-campus groups tend to support the judgments given by the senior students. Their hopes and expectations are not matched by their experience, and this shortfall is a cause of serious concern to them. While there is no reason to doubt the concern felt by the parents of students and by the college trustees, it is apparent that those who do not live and work on the campuses harbor a far more idealistic image of college community life than those who do. Much work remains to be done before such an image can be translated into reality.

SUMMARY

This chapter opened with the question, What is distinctive about our colleges? First of all, the colleges of the LCA are without apology church-related. This is clearly affirmed in the official documents of both synods and colleges, and it finds living expression in financial support, governance, and mutual service. In the midst of the structural ambiguity of American higher education, such clarity and vitality is in itself a notable mark of distinctiveness.

Because of this relationship, LCA colleges are able to proclaim their identity through the people who provide their leadership, the policies they establish, and the programs they conduct. As the survey attests, trustees and key administrators are chosen who place high value upon partnership with the church and upon goals which honor the Christian understanding of God and man. It is also apparent that these colleges have attracted faculty who, in large measure, affirm these goals and fulfill their teaching responsibilities with professional competence and personal concern for students.

As private institutions, they are free to undertake and support policies that emphasize strong academic programs, and also officially encourage the growth and expression of the Christian faith. Students are offered an educational experience that takes seriously all facets of human development, including the religious dimension. In the exercise of this freedom, church-related colleges serve as a safeguard against a monolithic secular system of higher education in the United States.

In their responses to the survey, constituents identify several program areas which contribute to the distinctive character of the LCA college. These include campus religious activities, the pastoral ministry of the chaplain, academic courses in religion, theological dialogue, education in values and moral responsibility, and the caring quality of campus community life. While no one of these is an exclusive province of church-related colleges, such colleges view programs of this kind as expressions of official institutional policy.

All LCA colleges are small, liberal arts, and residential in character. These descriptive qualities also connote distinctive characteristics which coincide with the educational goals of church-related colleges. Astin's study (1977),[6] for example, finds that students in smaller institutions are more likely to interact closely with faculty and find greater satisfaction in their classroom instructors. They are also more likely to experience an enhancement of their "interpersonal self-esteem," or their image of themselves as whole persons.

The significance of this is seen in the expectation which respondents from all constituency groups identify as their most highly valued goal, "Wholeness of Person." It is also with respect to this goal that many constituents feel their colleges are experiencing notable success. If these perceptions are indeed correct, colleges of the LCA are each year graduating large numbers of men and women who have developed qualities of personal wholeness, openness to learning, and sensitivity to cultural differences. Such graduates, and the colleges they represent, are in a position to make a distinctive and decisive contribution to American society in the 1980s.

6

Are Their Church Ties Healthy?

One of the startling conclusions reached by Earl McGrath (1977)[1] in his study of forty-eight Southern Baptist colleges and universities is that the future health of church-related educational institutions relates directly to being faithful to their declared allegiances. Without minimizing the role of national demographic and economic factors, he sees institutional distinctiveness as a major element in the continued viability of all independent colleges. Such distinctiveness, according to Edgar Carlson (1979),[2] is rarely embodied in college curricula but finds expression instead in ethnic or cultural qualities, including church-relatedness.

If McGrath's conclusion is valid, views on the ties between college and church may provide an index to the future vitality of LCA colleges. For this reason, survey data on these issues were sought with special eagerness on the part of persons carrying key responsibility for shaping the futures of the colleges.

Responses to the forty-six items in the survey instrument which probe attitudes on the subject of church relationships emerge as six contexts in which constituents evaluate the health of college-church relationships. Each context is identified by a question which focuses on a crucial issue:

- Is the college important to the mission of the church?
- Is there a growing separation between college and church?
- Should the church disengage itself from college support?
- Do people feel a sense of loyalty to their college?
- Do congregations lack an awareness of their college's importance?
- Is the college maintaining its distinctively Christian character?

In a sense these are "bottom line" questions. Expectations and perceptions of goals, programs, leadership, faculty, and students are all based on the assumption of an ongoing relationship between church and college, between respondent and institution. The question of strengths and weaknesses is secondary to the question of whether the whole enterprise is expendable or not. Only in this final segment are these ultimate options introduced.

Is the enterprise expendable or not? The answer from the constituents is unequivocal. LCA colleges are seen as an important aspect of the church's mission, and relations between the two partner institutions should be strengthened.

COLLEGES AND THE MISSION OF THE CHURCH

Variations may exist in constituents' understanding of the mission of the church. A church relationship with the college may be cherished for quite different reasons. Some may view their colleges as citadels for protecting youth from the temptations of the world. Others may see them as centers in which young people are prepared to become compassionate and responsible citizens of their communities. Such differences may indeed exist within the membership of the LCA. The 1976 LCA Partnership Statement accents a different mission when it emphasizes that the church sees its colleges as helping youth fulfill their sense of vocation in the world. Irrespective of people's concept of mission, however, 80 percent of the total sample affirm the role of the LCA colleges as important agencies through which the church can fulfill its mission. An impressive majority believes that the future survival of both church and college is dependent upon their continuing relationship.

Not all constituency groups, of course, share equally strong convictions on this question. Trustees, administrators, pastors, and Lutheran faculty, all of whom score significantly above the average of the total sample, feel most deeply that the church-related college fulfills an important and significant aspect of the church's mission. It should be highly gratifying to the leadership of the church that policymakers and leaders in those institutions see their work in this way. While the average response on this scale is quite strongly positive, the two student groups, freshmen and seniors, show the least willingness to affirm the importance of the college as a partner in the church's mission.

ARE COLLEGES AND CHURCHES
DRIFTING APART?

A second basic question in the context of college-church relationships was posed directly in the survey questionnaire: Is there a
growing separation between college and church? This is a question
which, if answered on the basis of the historical record, would un-
questionably call for an affirmative response. The history of American
higher education has indeed been the story of a growing separation
between colleges and the churches which were involved in their
beginnings.

In spite of this historical trend, most of the colleges of the LCA
have maintained their historic ties to the church. However, sharing as
they did with all of higher education in the impact of increased
enrollments resulting from government policies established between
1945 and 1970, they, too, were obliged to expand both faculties and
facilities to meet their public responsibilities. Preoccupied with these
physical demands and the increased governmental obligations that
accompanied programs for capital construction and student aid, some
colleges allowed their church relationships to deteriorate. As student
bodies and faculties grew, the percentage of Lutherans declined.
Fears were expressed in supporting synods that the church ties of
their college might be lost under the impact of expansion and secu-
larization. One LCA college, Hartwick, did indeed sever ties with its
sponsoring synod in 1968. Waterloo Lutheran University in Kitch-
ener, Ontario, facing insuperable fiscal problems, became a pro-
vincial institution in 1972, changing its name to Wilfred Laurier
University.

Against this historical background, it is understandable that the
question of a growing separation between college and church has
been frequently and pointedly raised within the Lutheran Church in
America, with the assumption that the college was doing the drifting.

Many loyal alumni saw the intimate character of their college crum-
bling as enrollments doubled and even tripled. The modern buildings
which sprang up overnight, dwarfing the mossy Old Mains and nos-
talgic fraternity houses, seemed to change the character of the college
as well as the appearance of the campus. At least some of the con-

75

cern expressed over the supposed "drifting away" from the church reflected a fear that the alma mater was simply growing too fast and that the "good old days" were gone forever.

While there is some factual basis for this concern, it must also be recognized that in these processes significant benefits accrued to the colleges of the LCA. Through generous financing by state and federal governments, outdated and often inadequate physical facilities were replaced. Modern classrooms, laboratories, and residence halls enabled the colleges to offer better academic programs. The expanded scope and quality of their course offerings equipped graduates to serve society in a greater variety of professions. Together with a large segment of American higher education, the LCA colleges "came of age" as modern academic institutions during these years. Thus, the same social forces which seemed to threaten many long-established forms and relationships cherished by both churches and colleges also served to expand the sphere of influence of these colleges, and hence also of the church.

In light of these historic trends and contemporary upheavals in the character of American higher education, however, the question had to be asked, Are the colleges growing away from the church? Indeed, it is one of the most critical questions in the entire study.

Since the survey sought to assess the images and expectations held by constituents of LCA colleges, the question was not posed in the historical context. For the respondents the question was: What about *my* college? Is *it* drifting farther and farther from the church?

Of the total sample of 6,728 persons, only 22 percent said yes, while 45 percent said no. A very substantial group, one-third of those polled, was unable to give a definitive reply, not feeling sufficiently informed or involved to make a judgment.

These data say it would not be appropriate either to dismiss as unimportant the concern over a growing separation or to magnify it as something that alarms college constituencies. The number who view the situation with concern is not great, and the number who discount its seriousness is twice as large. No individual group among the constituencies exhibits any significant variations in either direction from this general pattern of responses.

CHURCH DOLLARS FOR COLLEGES

A third grouping of items focuses upon several options relating to the financial support of its colleges. It is interesting that though a substantial number of persons do not feel sufficiently informed to respond to the question of whether or not their college is drifting away from the church, they are not reluctant to express an opinion on the desirability of the church's continuing support of its colleges. Though 33 percent of the respondents are uncertain as to whether or not their college is drifting away from the church, only 12 percent indicate uncertainty regarding the desirability of the church continuing its support of its colleges.

Moreover, the overwhelming weight of their substantive responses is to affirm the role of the church as a proper sponsor and supporter of colleges and universities. Of the 6,728 respondents, 77 percent disagree with the statement "Considering the many opportunities for its ministry, the church should consider the college among the less important places for its money." Ten percent indicate agreement. With regard to the statement "The church has fulfilled its obligation to higher education and should now disengage itself from support of its colleges," 80 percent disagree; only 7 percent agree.

It would be difficult to put the question of continued church support for colleges more clearly and simply than this. It would seem equally difficult, on the basis of these responses, to deny the strong desire of LCA college constituents for the continuance of a supportive relationship between the church and its colleges.

Even when the increased support of a campus ministry at non-church-related colleges and universities is posed as an alternative, the continued support of church colleges is solidly reaffirmed. Only 12 percent agree with the following statement, while 62 percent disagree: "In light of the substantial enrollment of Lutherans at state supported colleges and universities, financial support of the LCA should be shifted from its colleges to strengthening campus ministries at public institutions."

The suggestion is occasionally heard that the LCA might more effectively concentrate its resources on two or three colleges, with a view to making them outstanding, rather than on a large number of institutions of varying quality. This view receives small support; 13 percent agree, while 66 percent disagree.

While there are very few persons in any of the constituency groups who feel the church should disengage itself from its colleges, there are some notable variations of support among the groups. It is not surprising to find the college administrators, trustees, and Lutheran faculty most supportive of the church relationship. On the other hand, it is somewhat disturbing to discover that of all constituency groups, synod board members and LCA pastors are the most likely to favor the disengagement of church and college. It must quickly be added that the actual number of persons so disposed is small, but it is also true that individual members of these groups can be very influential in determining church policies and budgets, including those affecting colleges.

It is therefore significant that 12 percent of synod leaders and 11 percent of the pastors take the position that the church ought to discontinue completely its support of colleges. Only 3 percent of college administrators and 7 percent of the entire sample agree. A considerably greater discrepancy appears when the issue is posed not in terms of complete cessation of support but in terms of less support than is presently given. Twenty-three percent of synod leaders and 19 percent of the pastors feel the church should consider the colleges among the less important places for its money, while only 10 percent of the total sample express this opinion. Were they to choose between college support and support of ministries on campuses of non-church-related institutions, 29 percent of the pastors and 27 percent of synod board members would choose the campus ministries. In contrast, only 15 percent of the laity in the parishes, and 11 percent of the total sample, would agree with such a choice.

Even though all these percentage figures represent minority opinion critical of continued church support of its colleges, there is reason for concern when that minority is among those most influential in the formation of church policy. Even students, whose responses to many other questions appear to be quite critical of the church, are here more sympathetic to continued church support of colleges than are the pastors. The same is true of all groups of laity, parents of students, alumni, and even non-Lutheran faculty.

THE LOYALTY FACTOR

A fourth configuration of responses focuses on the question of loyalty to the college, its goals and purposes. Such a feeling finds expression in affirmative responses to a series of positive statements about the college. Although one-fourth of the persons sampled were not familiar enough with the college to venture either a positive or negative opinion, the strong majority registers favorable judgments on such statements as "I am well aware of the purpose and goals of my college," "The religious commitment of my college is clear and well-known to me," "I feel a sense of loyalty to my college and its future," "My college manages its financial resources well." Positive responses to these statements outweigh negative responses by at least three to one. On the specific question of personal loyalty to the college and its future, 76 percent of the total sample give favorable replies, and only 9 percent disagree.

The strongest convictions of loyalty are found among trustees, administrative leaders, and Lutheran faculty. Students, whether freshmen or seniors, are least likely to express such feelings toward their college.

More revealing, however, than the varying attitudes of loyalty among constituency groups is the importance of the age factor. The analysis indicates that the older the respondents, the greater the likelihood of expressed loyalty. Persons fifty-two years of age or older show the highest average score, well above the general average. The younger age-group, which includes all students and some representation from other groups as well, ranks lowest in expressions of loyalty.

What are we to make of this phenomenon? There is considerable evidence that an appreciation of the forces and factors which shape lives deepens with passing years. Many a youthful rebel has returned to thank a college professor or administrator whose expectations and decisions seemed at an earlier time to be unreasonable. Moreover, the 1960s and early 1970s were generally characterized by a spirit which questioned the values of all institutions, whether schools and colleges, churches or government, or even families.

Educational institutions, however, which ignore the seriousness of this questioning and the validity of some student criticisms of the "establishment," may have to face similar resistances in the future. Even today college students are not ready to accord their institutions the trust and loyalty which older generations were willing to give. A substantial burden therefore rests upon the colleges to direct their policies and programs for the primary benefit of their students. Special efforts also are needed to demonstrate and interpret to younger alumni and congregational laity the usefulness and social significance of church-related colleges.

Should one require further evidence of the loyalty affirmed by a substantial majority of all respondents, the "acid test" would be their readiness to increase personal financial support of their colleges. Of students in the sample, 34 percent declare themselves ready to increase their personal financial support of their colleges. An additional 26 percent are undecided, and 12 percent do not know. Only one out of four in the entire sampling of 6,728 persons of all eleven constituency groups say they would not increase their personal financial support of their church-related college.

The groups most closely identified with the college (administrative leaders, trustees, and Lutheran faculty) are the most willing to increase their giving. More significant, however, are the strongly affirming responses from groups especially close to the church: Lutheran alumni, LCA pastors, and synod boards. Of these, nearly 45 percent express a readiness to increase their contributions in support of their colleges. It is the laity in congregations who display most reserve or reluctance in answering this question. More than 50 percent register either an "undecided" or "don't know" response. Their answers may reflect a lack of both information and understanding concerning the colleges, a condition which is clearly documented in other data from the survey.

In the structure of the LCA, a primary channel of financial support to the college is an annual synodical appropriation. Each of the thirty-three synods is related to at least one college, for whose "material welfare" the synod constitutions affirm responsibility. The size of these annual operational grants varies with the size and resources of the synod and the vitality of its relationship with its college. Since 1968 the synodical support of LCA colleges has declined steadily, from $3,229,009 in 1968, to $2,442,129 in 1978, a drop of 24.4 percent. During these same years, annual expenditures of the colleges have increased from $73,499,000 to $137,203,000, or 86.7 percent. Synodical support of colleges as a percentage of total institutional expenditures dropped from 4.4 percent in 1968 to 1.8 percent in 1978. As a percentage of total synodical expenditures, college support dropped from 9.0 percent in 1968 to 5.1 percent in 1978, while regular synodical expenditures rose by 33.8 percent.

In view of these trends in college support, the response of constituents to a specific survey question concerning the future is especially instructive: The direct financial support of my college by the church should be:

Substantially increased	16%
Moderately increased	30%
Maintained at present levels	18%
Moderately reduced	3%
Eliminated entirely	2%
Don't know	30%

Virtually no sentiment was registered by the constituencies either for the reduction of or elimination of church support for colleges. The strongest voice suggests either a moderate or a substantial increase, while two-thirds of all respondents favor either an increase or the maintenance of present support levels.

The sharp discrepancy between responses to this survey and the actual trends of college support during the past decade in the LCA calls for some inquiry and further analysis. It is, of course, to be expected that groups closest to the college would want financial support increased. More significant is the strong support found among pastors, 50 percent of whom favor an increase. Another 26 percent wish to maintain present levels of church support. Members of synod boards declare similar sentiments, 43 percent favoring increased support and 35 percent favoring the maintenance of present support levels. Only one out of ten favors a moderate reduction, and 7.7 percent feel church support of colleges should be terminated.

Substantial percentages of laity, parents and students, ranging from 35 percent to 50 percent, do not feel well enough informed on the issue of church support to venture an opinion. Of those who do, however, virtually all favor increasing church support or maintaining it at current levels.

In view of a preference profile such as this, it is difficult to account for the persistent decline in budgeted church support of colleges during the past decade.

The failure of benevolence support from congregations to keep pace with annual inflation has resulted in some restraints on all churchwide and synodical programs. Synods have become increasingly involved in a variety of service programs to congregations, pastors, and communities, most of which have required budgetary support. Strong personal advocacy of these programs has brought positive response from synod leadership, while the more conventional institutional programs, traditionally the recipients of the largest synodical grants, have received less attention. As resources lagged, the larger institutional grants gradually have been pared to provide funding for programs of more immediate priority. The rationale for reduction of college support has been based on the assumption that additional funding sources are more readily available to colleges than to other church-related activities.

It is also true that synodical structures rarely provide committees directly responsible for the interpretation, support, and even advocacy of the college which the synod supports. The election of members to the college board of trustees by the synod does not serve this purpose. Once elected, these persons see themselves as related to the college rather than to the synod. A synod committee, with special responsibility for interpreting the college and encouraging its support within the synod, would be of great benefit to both synod and college. In cooperation with the college, such a committee could be most helpful in overcoming the lack of information and understanding among congregational laity so frequently attested to in their responses to the survey. It also might provide opportunity to articulate before the synod the long-range importance of its institutional programs, and to note that continuing and increased support is favored by the strong majority of pastors, synod board members, and informed laity in the congregations of the LCA.

RELATIONS WITH CONGREGATIONS

One of the conditions affecting college-church relationships most clearly attested to by the survey is the need among congregational members for a fuller knowledge and understanding of their colleges. These congregations are the source of church support, both financial and spiritual, and in them is probably the richest untapped resource for student recruitment in the 1980s. At the present time, about 7,000 Lutheran students are enrolled in the eighteen colleges of the LCA, slightly more than an average of one student per LCA congregation.

Virtually every group represented in the survey expresses a strong opinion that members of congregations lack an awareness of the contribution of their colleges. This assessment is especially significant among the groups largely or entirely related to Lutheran congregations. Of the laity, 70 percent admit they are not as well informed as they should be, but at the same time almost the same percentage soundly rejects the idea that there is little need for the college and its support. Nor do the laity attribute to their pastors any lack of conviction when they address their congregations on the subject of college support.

It appears that there is in the congregations of the LCA a general awareness that colleges are needed, along with a readiness to receive information about the colleges and their role in the mission of the church.

Pastors also affirm strongly their congregation's lack of awareness concerning the contribution of its colleges, but they apparently misjudge the sentiments of members concerning the need for the college and its support. While 38 percent of pastors and synod board members express the opinion that the congregation see little need for the colleges, only 13 percent of the laity share this view, and 70 percent register the opposite view.

Some explanation of this misunderstanding of lay sentiment may be found in the clergy's evaluation of their own relationship with the college of their synod. Almost half of them do not feel they have a close relationship with their synod's college. This is especially regrettable, in view of the fact that of all the constituent groups, pastors express the greatest degree of eagerness for activities which will encourage greater understanding between church and college. College leadership, which is least aware of the lack of college information in the congregations, would do well to direct much more attention to both congregations and pastors. There is clearly a climate of receptivity on the part of both. During the critical decade ahead, the informed and enthusiastic support of pastors and congregations may constitute one of the most important resources for the colleges of the LCA.

The desire for closer relationships between church and college, however, is not confined to the clergy. In evaluating an extended series of items describing activities which could assist such relationships, nine persons out of ten in the entire sample respond favorably. Clearly there is a strong desire among the constituencies of LCA colleges for reciprocal efforts toward closer college-church relationships.

Among the specific actions indicated as desirable in achieving this goal are dialogue between pastors and professors; discussion of the mutual statements of intent between colleges and synods; college contacts with congregations through publications, visiting groups, and special speakers; encouragement by the church of qualified members of congregations to seek enrollment at LCA colleges; expressions of strong college support by influential clergy and by church leadership; employment of a careful nominating process by the synod to encourage the election of able and dedicated college trustees; the clear affirmation of a church relationship in the catalog and other documents of the college; and a more vigorous role on the part of trustees in interpreting the college to their church constituency.

One of the specific hallmarks of the Christian character of the college which wins strong support (65 percent) throughout the survey is that most faculty should be professing Christians. The predominantly Lutheran-related constituencies give this expectation even stronger than average support (77 percent). The active implementation of this policy by the colleges might therefore be seen as contributory to a greater degree of confidence in college-church relations. While insisting upon the importance of respect for an institutional commitment to the Christian faith, Lutheran constituents, pastors included, also strongly support the freedom of students and faculty to express agnostic or anti-Christian positions. It is somewhat surprising that only one-half of these same groups favor a required religion course oriented toward biblical literature. On the basis of these responses, it seems clear that Lutheran constituents do not expect their colleges to become either parochial or sectarian as the price for closer relationships with the church. The expectations and the opportunities lie in the development of improved personal relationships and more imaginative and purposeful communication on the part of both the college and the church.

Epilogue: What Lies Ahead?

As the decade of the 1980s begins, the air is filled with predictions and prophecies concerning the future of American higher education. Declining enrollments, spiraling costs, and increasing governmental control loom as ominous factors in an uncertain future for all colleges and universities. Church-related colleges share these uncertainties and are, in fact, in a more vulnerable position than the heavily subsidized public institutions. At the same time, they possess certain inherent strengths which may enable them to cope more effectively than many public institutions with the difficult circumstances ahead.

It seems appropriate in concluding a survey of expectations and perceptions of LCA colleges by their constituents that two additional questions be raised: How will these hazards of the 1980s affect the colleges of the LCA? What are the positive factors which provide encouragement for them in the future?

Of most immediate concern for all small colleges are the national population trends. The decade of the 1980s will be one of significant decline in the number of eighteen-year-olds in the United States, the age-group from which colleges have normally drawn most of their students. The number will decline 26.4 percent between the years 1978–79 and 1991–92. In some areas of the country the percentage of decline will be even greater and will be further augmented by an out-migration of people. Northern states are expected to experience the decline most pointedly—not a promising sign for the colleges of the LCA, most of which are concentrated in those states.

Projections of this kind raise warning flags for LCA colleges and point to the necessity for careful planning. There is actually no reason why most institutions, if otherwise healthy, cannot function with fewer students, provided they can reduce their operating costs commensurately. It will be essential for all colleges to develop optional plans for the 1980s, with enough flexibility built into staffing patterns to enable them to handle various levels of enrollment. An unwillingness to take predictions seriously and to develop such contingency plans for enrollment decline may be the formula for early institutional demise in the 1980s.

Closely related to the enrollment decline will be the effects of persisting inflation. All of higher education will share this problem. However, the private sector, depending heavily on student tuition for its operational income, will feel it especially in the widening gap between its fees and those of tax-supported institutions.

It is likely that the scope of federal and state subsidies, both through student aid and institutional grants, will be broadened to embrace more and more of the private sector. The public commitment to higher education will not be withdrawn, and together with heavy financial support will go increased government control—a phenomenon which developed to an alarming degree during the 1970s. Loss of institutional autonomy may be the price of survival for many colleges and universities.

In spite of the uncertainties of the coming decade, there are nevertheless significant signs of strength, both within the church-related colleges themselves and in the recognition they are receiving from the general public. Edgar Carlson has reminded us of the key role played by church-related colleges in preserving diversity in the American system of higher education.[1] Beyond this, the growing public concern for the recovery of values and for moral and spiritual growth can best be met by institutions whose professed goals and programs are directed to these ends.

This may be the greatest asset of the church-related sector as it enters the 1980s. It is surely its greatest opportunity for the kind of service to society which both the church and the LCA colleges see as essential reasons for their existence. The series of reaffirmations by individual denominations and colleges during the 1970s and, finally, by the twenty-three denominations jointly represented in the National Congress of Church-Related Colleges and Universities in Washington in February 1980 signals a readiness to seize the opportunity in the coming decade.[2]

In the reassessment of higher education induced by the decline of public confidence during the 1970s, the style and pattern of education most familiar to the church-related colleges has been judged by

Alexander Astin to be the most effective form of education available to undergraduates in this country. The qualities of bigness, impersonality, anonymity, and overspecialization, which have been the focus of such sharp criticism by students and others, have not been generally characteristic of church-related institutions. Most of them are small, residential liberal arts colleges which, according to Astin's studies, do the best job of educating undergraduate students.[3]

That this awareness is shared by parents and students is evidenced by the fact that in spite of higher tuition, the enrollments of private colleges actually have increased by 13 percent during the past ten years.[4] This is not to say that such increases will persist in the face of general population trends and predictions of decline. But it suggests that if church-related colleges will remain faithful to their character and stated educational goals, they have a product which is both needed and will be increasingly sought after in the coming decade.

There is thus far no evidence to support the frequently expressed contention that church-related colleges have been closing in great numbers in recent years. A study sponsored by the National Institute of Independent Colleges and Universities in 1978 showed that a total of 171 private colleges closed or merged between 1970 and 1978.[5] Forty-three percent of these were Roman Catholic institutions, most of them with fewer than 250 students. Most of the others had no active church affiliation. Only a few were associated with main-line religious denominations. Moreover, while these schools were closing, their places were being taken by new institutions, so that the net decrease was actually 65, rather than 171.

In view of the massive problems looming in the 1980s, it would be idle to suppose that there will be no casualties among LCA colleges. Not all will believe the signs of the times and plan for careful consolidation of resources. Some will be victimized by social and economic factors that even good planning cannot overcome. But when the decade of the 1980s has run its course, most of the present LCA institutions will still be offering their educational opportunities to students.

It should be remembered that many of the same economic and social problems which confront the colleges also confront the church and its congregations. It is therefore also possible that the church may be unable to continue its financial support to all of its presently related institutions and may be obliged, however reluctantly, to withdraw its support from some of them.

As the colleges and the church face the future as partners in tasks of higher education, there are plans they should be formulating and steps they should be undertaking together in order to maintain this crucial ministry. The declining numbers of college-age youth does not constitute a problem for the colleges alone. It constitutes a potential leadership crisis for all of society, including the church. There will most certainly be a shortage of young leaders in the 1990s, and there will be keen competition for those who are most able. The church will be wise to see its colleges as a resource for its own leadership, but also for the kind of compassionate, wise, and socially motivated leadership it covets for society.

There are some things the colleges will need to do themselves. Wise and frugal management is essential, together with long-range plans embodying viable options to meet changing circumstances. Constitutional documents and policy statements need to be carefully reviewed to prevent unnecessary and costly litigation. It may even be necessary for colleges in the 1980s to maintain legal counsel on their staffs, either full-time or in combination with other administrative or academic duties. Clear and unambiguous statements of faculty policies and practices—vigorous development programs which reach beyond special campaigns, incorporating a strong emphasis on deferred giving—and imaginative programs of student recruitment, not overlooking the cultivation of Lutheran congregations as important resources, are needed.

Remembering the counsel of Astin and McGrath and others,[6] LCA colleges will do well to make conscious efforts in the 1980s to reaffirm and strengthen their identity as church-related institutions. Without a clearly defined identity, chances of survival are limited. Publications and public events of the college should reflect it. So also should campus symbolism, financial aid policies, and procedures for the selection of faculty and administrative staff.

There are also things which the church can do as it looks toward the future in partnership with its colleges. Results of the survey of images and expectations make it abundantly clear that a strong desire exists among the colleges, congregations, and clergy to maintain and deepen the relationship between church and college. Moreover, the constitutions of the LCA and each of its synods expressly mandate the support of church-related colleges.[7]

This coincidence of obligation and desire could find expression in serious cooperative explorations by church and college leadership, or through a churchwide consulting committee, on ways of more effective use of college resources by the church. These might include not merely the use of facilities for conventions or committee meetings, but also commissioned studies and research in areas of special concern to the church in its efforts to serve its own needs and those of society. Virtually untapped resources for such purposes are available among college faculties, in the persons of economists, sociologists, specialists in business management, government, international affairs, and teachers of foreign languages, to name only a few.

Beyond their potential as supportive resources for internal programs of the church, the colleges should be viewed by the church within the context of the Lutheran understanding of Christian vocation. The colleges offer young men and women both the opportunity and the resources to develop their capacities for the fullest expression of their calling as Christians in the world through a variety of professions and activities. A renewed emphasis on this aspect of higher education in the 1980s would be especially realistic in view of the anticipated shortage of leadership. In the spirit of the Partnership Statement, it would also strengthen the bond between the church and the colleges in their common concern for the well-being of both church and society.

There is no doubt that the 1980s will require special efforts by the colleges to recruit students. The church could provide enormous assistance in these efforts by intentionally encouraging its college-age youth to enroll in colleges of the LCA. Each year about 57,000 young men and women, members of LCA congregations, graduate from high schools. More than half of them go on to college. Yet only about 1,500, or one in nineteen, enrolls in an LCA college.

While it is true that tuition charges at most private colleges are considerably higher than those of tax-supported institutions, it is not necessarily true that the total expense for a college year will be greater. Board, room, and books will not vary greatly, and personal expenditures will depend upon available resources, wherever a student may be. Financial aid programs at LCA colleges are able in many cases to equalize the cost differentials.

In 1979, 69 percent of all students attending LCA colleges received financial aid, in proportion to documented need. The average aid package for the year for all students, including Lutherans, was $2,500. With such assistance available through the colleges, from public sources and from the college's own resources, no member of a Lutheran congregation who can demonstrate need should hesitate to seek admission. Pastors and youth leaders should encourage prospective students and their parents to take this first step of applying to an LCA college—or at least conversing personally with a college director of admissions—before concluding that the costs are prohibitive.

On the basis of the survey outcomes which have been presented in this book, the colleges of the LCA should enter the 1980s with renewed confidence. The educational goals which they have established have been strongly endorsed by their constituents. Their efforts to fulfill the goals have been generally commended, both by those directly involved in the educational process and by outside observers. Some areas have been identified as needing improvement.

As they look to the future, with constituencies supportive of their goals and pleased with them as partners, they will be well advised to proclaim the solidarity of their partnership with the church. For its part, the Lutheran Church in America has given its assurance that its primary expectation in this partnership is that its related colleges and universities perform their tasks as educational institutions of integrity, with wisdom, compassion, and skill. By so doing they will both honor God and serve his creation.

Notes

Preface

1. Actually, eleven separate surveys were carried out on randomly selected samples of the eleven constituency groups, using identical procedures for the collection of data. Six of the groups showed percentages of participation that were 58 percent or higher. Five groups fell below this arbitrary standard. Samples of nonrespondents were secured from the five groups falling below a 58 percent response—seniors (50 percent), parents of freshmen (48 percent), parents of seniors (47 percent), alumni (44 percent), and congregational laity (30 percent)—to determine whether or not nonrespondents differ from respondents in how they view their college. Comparisons showed that both answered alike, attesting to the fact that these samples provide adequate estimates of how the five constituency groups view their college.

A full report of the literature review that preceded the study, the research methodology used in carrying out the study, and the actual research findings in tabular form are available in the following publications:

Daniel O. Aleshire, *Technical Manual for the Research Report to the Joint Committee of the Division for Mission in North America and the Council of the LCA Colleges on A Survey of Images and Expectations of LCA Colleges* (Minneapolis: Youth Research Center, 1976).

Charles R. Bruning, *Relationships between Church-Related Colleges and Their Constituencies* (New York: Lutheran Church in America, 1975).

Merton P. Strommen, *Research Report to the Joint Committee of the Division for Mission in North America and the Council of the LCA Colleges on A Survey of Images and Expectations of LCA Colleges* (New York: Lutheran Church in America, 1976).

Chapter 1

1. Manning M. Pattillo and Donald M. Mackenzie, *Church-Sponsored Higher Education in the United States* (Washington: American Council on Education, 1966), p. 5.

2. Robert Rue Parsonage, ed., *Church-Related Higher Education* (Valley Forge: Judson Press, 1978), p. 292.

3. W. Vance Grant and C. George Lind, *Digest of Education Statistics 1979* (Washington: Department of Health, Education and Welfare, National Center for Education Statistics, 1979), p. 84.

4. Pattillo and Mackenzie, *Church-Sponsored Higher Education*, pp. 191–97.

5. C. Robert Pace, *Education and Evangelism* (New York: McGraw-Hill, 1972), pp. 21–23.

6. Merrimon Cunninggim, "Varieties of Church Relatedness," in Parsonage, *Church-Related Higher Education,* p. 38.

7. Ibid., p. 74.

8. Brief historical accounts of the development of Lutheranism in America may be found in Sidney Ahlstrom, *A Religious History of the American People* (New Haven: Yale University Press, 1972), and Conrad Bergendoff, *The Church of the Lutheran Reformation* (St. Louis: Concordia Publishing House, 1967).

9. Cunninggim, "Varieties of Church Relatedness," pp. 35–38.

10. Statistical data on LCA colleges may be found in *LCA Yearbook.* The Department for Higher Education, LCA, also assembles extensive data from LCA colleges each year and maintains trends studies in a variety of areas.

11. "A Statement of the Lutheran Church in America: The Basis for Partnership between Church and College" (New York: Lutheran Church in America, 1976). Copies are available on request from the Department for Higher Education, Division for Mission in North America, Lutheran Church in America, 231 Madison Avenue, New York, NY 10016.

12. Most of the LCA colleges have published histories which provide the full story of their development.

Chapter 2

1. Alexander W. Astin, "On the Failures of Educational Policy," *Change,* September 1977, pp. 40–43.

2. *The Purposes and Performance of Higher Education in the United States Approaching the Year 2000,* A Report and Recommendations by the Carnegie Commission on Higher Education (New York: McGraw-Hill, 1973), pp. 43–52.

3. Alexander W. Astin, *Four Critical Years* (San Francisco: Jossey-Bass, 1977), pp. 6–7.

4. Merton P. Strommen, Milo L. Brekke, Ralph C. Underwager, and Arthur L. Johnson, *A Study of Generations* (Minneapolis: Augsburg Publishing House, 1972), p. 44.

Chapter 3

1. The complete summary of this study will appear in the published documents of the National Congress of Church-Related Colleges and Universities.

2. These booklets have been compiled in a volume entitled *Servant Leadership* (New York: Paulist Press, 1977).

Chapter 4

1. Trend analyses are made by the LCA Department for Higher Education on the basis of annual data reports.

2. The clusters of items which identify the three expectations of fac-

ulty were derived empirically by factor analysis. The reason the items intercorrelate to form each factor is that respondents are guided in their answers by certain pervasive constructs or expectations. Here the consistency of responses clearly indicates the presence of these expectations: Competence as Teachers, Commitment to Educational Mission, and Christian Commitment.

3. This analytic procedure, called AID (Automatic Interaction Detection), developed in 1974, explores the data to identify the variables which account for the greatest amount of variance. This procedure, used on the faculty sample of 857 persons, supplied the information reported here. The *Research Report, A Survey of Images and Expectations of LCA Colleges,* pp. 142–54, describes how the variables, isolated through the analyses, structured the sample's response to the following dependent variables: Growing Separation between Church and College, Church Disengagement from College Support, and Seeking Mutuality between College and Church.

Chapter 5

1. Charles McCoy, *The Responsible Campus* (Nashville: Board of Education, The United Methodist Church, 1972), p. 19.

2. Christopher Jencks and David Riesman, *The Academic Revolution* (New York: Doubleday and Co., 1968), p. 322.

3. Cunninggim, "Varieties of Church Relatedness," p. 86.

4. Ibid., p. 85.

5. pp. 12–13.

6. Astin, *Four Critical Years,* pp. 231, 240.

Chapter 6

1. Earl McGrath, *Study of Southern Baptist Colleges and Universities* (Nashville: The Education Commission of the Southern Baptist Convention, 1977), p. 20.

2. Edgar M. Carlson, "The Future of Church-Related Higher Education," an address delivered at California Lutheran College, October 12, 1979.

Epilogue

1. Edgar M. Carlson, *The Future of Church-Related Higher Education* (Minneapolis: Augsburg Publishing House, 1977), p. 66.

2. A series of "Affirmations" was prepared as a working document for the meeting of the National Congress of Church-Related Colleges and Universities in Washington, D.C., February 1–2, 1980.

3. Astin, *Four Critical Years,* pp. 244–45.

4. Howard R. Bowen and W. John Minter, *Independent Higher Education,* 1978 (Washington: National Association of Independent Colleges and Universities, 1978), p. 9.

5. Virginia Ann Fadil and Julianne Still Thrift, *Openings, Closings, Mergers and Accreditation Status of Independent Colleges and Universi-*

ties Winter 1970 through Summer 1978 (Washington: National Institute of Independent Colleges and Universities, 1978), pp. 1–33.

6. Earl McGrath, *Study of Southern Baptist Colleges and Universities,* p. 20.

7. *LCA Constitution,* Article VIII, Section 8c(2), and *Approved Constitution for Synods,* Article Seven, Section 2.

Bibliography

The following list of books and other reference material is not intended to be comprehensive. It includes only selected sources which have been used as references in the preparation of this book. The major source is the *Research Report, A Survey of Images and Expectations of LCA Colleges* by Merton A. Strommen.

A College-Related Church: United Methodist Perspectives. Nashville: National Commission on United Methodist Higher Education, 1976.

"A Statement of the Lutheran Church in America: The Basis for Partnership between Church and College." New York: Lutheran Church in America, 1976.

Ahlstrom, Sidney. *A Religious History of the American People*. New Haven: Yale University Press, 1972.

Aleshire, Daniel O. *Technical Manual for the Research Report to the Joint Committee of the Division for Mission in North America and the Council of the LCA Colleges on A Survey of Images and Expectations of LCA Colleges*. Minneapolis: Youth Research Center, 1976.

Astin, Alexander W. *Four Critical Years*. San Francisco: Jossey-Bass, 1977.

————. "On the Failures of Educational Policy," *Change*, September 1977, pp. 40–43.

Baepler, Richard, et al. *The Quest for a Viable Saga*. Valparaiso: Association of Lutheran College Faculties, 1977.

Bergendoff, Conrad. *The Church of the Lutheran Reformation*. St. Louis: Concordia Publishing House, 1967.

Bowen, Howard R., and Minter, W. John. *Independent Higher Education, 1978*. Washington, D.C.: National Association of Independent Colleges and Universities, 1978.

Bruning, Charles R. *Relationships between Church-Related Colleges and Their Constituencies*. New York: Lutheran Church in America, 1975.

Carlson, Edgar M. *Church-Sponsored Higher Education and the Lutheran Church in America*. New York: Board of College Education and Church Vocations, Lutheran Church in America, 1967.

————. *The Future of Church-Related Colleges*. Minneapolis: Augsburg Publishing House, 1977.

Church and State: A Lutheran Perspective. New York: Board of Social Ministry, Lutheran Church in America, 1963.

Cunninggim, Merrimon. "Varieties of Church-Relatedness in Higher Education," in Robert Rue Parsonage, *Church-Related Higher Education*. Valley Forge: Judson Press, 1978, pp. 17–101.

Fadil, Virginia Ann, and Thrift, Julianne Still. *Openings, Closings, Merg-*

ers and Accreditation Status of Independent Colleges and Universities Winter 1970 through Summer 1978. Washington: National Institute of Independent Colleges and Universities, 1978.

Gamelin, Francis C. Church-Related Identity of Lutheran Colleges. Washington: Lutheran Educational Conference of North America, 1975.

Grant, W. Vance, and Lind, C. George. Digest of Education Statistics 1979. Washington: U.S. Department of Health, Education and Welfare, National Center for Education Statistics, 1979.

Greenleaf, Robert K. Servant Leadership. New York: Paulist Press, 1977.

Jencks, C   , and Riesman, David. The ademic Revolution. New Y   Doubleday and Co., 1968.

McCoy, Charles. The Responsible Campus. Nashville: Board of Education, The United Methodist Church, 1972.

McGrath, Earl. Study of Southern Baptist Colleges and Universities. Nashville: The Education Commission of the Southern Baptist Convention, 1977.

"The Mission of LCA Colleges and Universities." New York: Board of College Education and Church Vocations, Lutheran Church in America, 1969.

Olsen, Arthur L., ed. Cooperation for the Future. Washington: Lutheran Educational Conference of North America, 1976.

Pace, C. Robert. Education and Evangelism: A Profile of Protestant Colleges. Carnegie Commission on Higher Education Study. New York: McGraw-Hill, 1972.

Pattillo, Manning M., and Mackenzie, Donald M. Church-Sponsored Higher Education in the United States. Washington: American Council on Education, 1966.

Parsonage, Robert Rue, ed. Church-Related Higher Education. Valley Forge: Judson Press, 1978.

Pfnister, Allan O. Trends in Higher Education in the United States: A Review of the Literature. Washington: Lutheran Educational Conference of North America, 1976.

The Purposes and the Performance of Higher Education in the United States Approaching the Year 2000: A Report and Recommendations by the Carnegie Commission on Higher Education. New York: McGraw-Hill, 1973.

Strommen, Merton P.; Brekke, Milo L.; Underwager, Ralph C.; and Johnson, Arthur L. A Study of Generations. Minneapolis: Augsburg Publishing House, 1972.

Strommen, Merton P. Research Report to the Joint Committee of the Division for Mission in North America and the Council of the LCA Colleges on A Survey of Images and Expectations of LCA Colleges. New York: Lutheran Church in America, 1976.

————. "Images and Expectations of LCA Colleges," in Papers and Proceedings of the Lutheran Educational Conference of North America, 1977. Washington, D.C., 1977.